PRAC
GOU

Comp
Coming
®

Cast Iron
Cooking

Paré • Billey • Pirk • Darcy

Distributed by
Canada Book Distributors
www.canadabookdistributors.com
www.companyscoming.com
Tel: 1-800-661-9017

Library and Archives Canada Cataloguing in Publication

Title: Cast iron cooking / Paré, Billey, Pirk, Darcy
Other titles: Company's coming
Names: Paré, Jean, 1927- author. | Billey, Ashley, author. | Pirk, Wendy, 1973- author. | Darcy, James, 1956- author.
Description: Includes index.
Identifiers: Canadiana 20210370890 | ISBN 9781990534003 (softcover)
Subjects: LCSH: Cast-iron cookware. | LCSH: Cooking. | LCGFT: Cookbooks.
Classification: LCC TX657.C37 P37 2022 | DDC 641.5/89—dc23

All cover photos by Company's Coming except: from GettyImages: bhofack2, ginauf, wmaster890, Vladlenaazima, Bojsha65, Polina Shurygina.

All inside photos by Company's Coming except: from GettyImages: 500, 125; A.K. Butler, 157; AlexeyBorodin, 79; bgsmith, 19; bhofack2, 15, 61, 83, 115, 135; carpaumar, 49; Liudmyla Chuhunova, 73; CowlickCreative, 105; dlerick, 133; fortyforks, 65; freeskyline, 93; ginauf, 111; CP Hoffman, 143; istetiana, 11; Iamthatiam, 137; kellyvandellen, 99; Lauren King, 113; Panagiotis Kyriakos, 13; Jen Lobo, 91; Bartosz Luczak, 141; margouillatphotos, 127; MarkSkalny, 95; MihailUlianikov, 5; Lynne Mitchell, 57, 103; MSPhotographic, 47, 67; nata_vkusidey, 153; OksanaKiian, 97, 119; OlyaSolodenko, 77; Petroos, 149; picalotta, 155; rez-art, 53; ronniechua, 87; Sarsmis, 117; scottiebumich, 6; Scukrov, 107; Polina Shurygina, 1, 39; Ihor Smishko, 75; Carlos Valle, 41; VeselovaElena, 59; Tatiana Volgutova, 63, 69; frederique wacquier, 151; wmaster890, 43, 71; Marie Wurm, 109; zi3000, 89; zefirchik06, 101; Zoryanchik, 21, 45. .

We acknowledge the financial support of the Government of Canada.
Nous reconnaissons l'appui financier du gouvernement du Canada.

Funded by the Government of Canada
Financé par le gouvernement du Canada | Canadä

PC: 38-1

Table of Contents

The Jean Paré Story

Jean Paré, the founder of Company's Coming, grew up understanding that the combination of family, friends and home cooking is the best recipe for a good life.

Jean has mentored and inspired her team of chefs and cooks to embrace her ideals and approach to recipe creation based on tried-and-true testing.

"Never share a recipe you wouldn't use yourself."

Early in her career, Jean volunteered to prepare a dinner for more than 1,000 people attending the 50th anniversary celebration of the Vermillion School of Agriculture, now Lakeland College. From there, she launched a flourishing catering operation.

As requests for her recipes increased, Jean was often asked, "Why don't you write a cookbook?" The release of 150 Delicious Squares on April 14, 1981, marked the debut of what would soon turn into one of the world's most popular cookbook series, now with more than 350 titles.

Company's Coming cookbooks are distributed in Canada, the United States and other world markets. Bestsellers many times over in English, Company's Coming cookbooks have also been published in French and Spanish.

Familiar and trusted in home kitchens around the world, Company's Coming cookbooks are offered in a variety of formats. Highly regarded as kitchen workbooks, the softcover Original Series, with its lay-flat comb binding, is still a favourite among home cooks.

Jean Paré's approach to cooking has always called for quick and easy recipes using everyday ingredients. That view served her well, and the tradition continues in the Practical Gourmet series. The chefs in our test kitchens have been inspired by Jean's leadership and guidance to carry on her passion for sharing great recipes with home cooks.

Jean's Golden Rule of Cooking is: *Never share a recipe you wouldn't use yourself. It's an approach that has worked—millions of times over!*

Introduction

For centuries, cast iron cookware was the most common type of cookware in the world. It has even been said that cast iron cookware is the oldest metal cooking utensil still being used today.

The casting technique for cast iron originated in China and was well established by the sixth century. Molten metal was poured into a sand mold (or "cast"), and once the metal cooled and hardened, the mold was broken to remove the cast iron pan, which was one solid piece, including the handle. The pan was then polished to a smooth surface. The process has remained largely unchanged even today, except machines instead of people now pour the molten metal into the molds.

Cast iron cookware was used to cook over open flames long before ovens were invented. From China, the casting technique spread to other parts of Asia and Europe, and by medieval times, heavy 3-legged cast iron cauldrons, utensils, kettles and all shapes of pots hung over fires inside at hearths or outside over campfires throughout Europe.

Early European immigrants then brought cast iron cookware to the Americas. Cast iron Dutch ovens were the norm for pioneers trekking west across what is now the United States, as well as for chuckwagon cooks that fed the cowboys on their long cattle drives.

Cast iron frying pans were an essential tool for prospectors in California and the Yukon during the gold rushes. The Lodge brand of cast iron cookware, created by Joseph Lodge, is the longest running cast iron manufacturer in the U.S., dating back to 1896 (though the original foundry, called Blackrock, burned down in 1910 and was rebuilt and renamed Lodge).

Cast iron cookware began to lose popularity in the early 1900s, when aluminum cookware became more widely available. Aluminum was attractive to consumers because it was less expensive and much lighter than the heavy, cumbersome cast iron pots and pans. By the late 1900s and early 2000s, however, aluminum cookware also fell out of favour, and non-stick skillets became the most common type of cookware in North American.

Today, although many cooks use stainless steel or non-stick cookware, cast iron is making a comeback and retaking its rightful place in kitchens around the globe.

Benefits

So why is cast iron cookware currently enjoying a resurgence in popularity? For starters, it is convenient. You can start your dish on the stovetop and finish it in the oven in the same pan. And who doesn't love the rustic appeal of sizzling fajitas or a steak served from a cast iron skillet?

More importantly, it is extremely durable. When properly cared for, cast iron cookware can last more than a lifetime. In the past, it was common for cast iron pots and pans to be passed down from generation to generation. Unless it is cracked or warped, there is not much you can do to ruin a cast iron pot or pan. Even the rustiest old skillet can be cleaned up, re-seasoned and used again.

In fact, cast iron cookware improves with use. Unlike aluminum, stainless steel or non-stick cookware, whose performance can deteriorate with age, especially when used over high heat, cast iron pots and pans perform better with more use. Every time you cook with cast iron, you add to and strengthen the seasoning, protecting your cookware from rusting and helping to prevent your food from sticking.

One of the main reasons top chefs love cast iron is its ability to retain heat. Cast iron takes longer to heat up than aluminum or stainless steel, but once it is hot, it stays that way much longer. With other types of cookware, heat is lost when you add to the pan the food you want to cook. Cast iron, however, retains heat, resulting in better browning and searing.

Temperatures for Cast Iron cookware °F/°C	
Low	150/65
Medium-low	225/110
Medium	300/150
Medium-high	375/190
High	425/220

Another boon of cast iron is that once it is well seasoned, it is naturally non-stick. Other non-stick cookware relies on chemical coatings that have been linked to health issues, especially when used at high heat or when the coating begins to degrade. With a well-seasoned cast iron pan, your food slides out easily.

Caring for Cast Iron

One of the reasons cast iron fell out of popularity is because it got a reputation for being difficult to care for. True, your cast iron cookware needs a little more attention than stainless steel or aluminum pots and pans, but caring for cast iron is not nearly as difficult as some people believe it to be.

What is seasoning?

That lovely black finish, or patina, you see on the cooking surface of well-used cast iron pots and skillets is the seasoning—a layer of oil that has been cooked onto and bonded with the iron surface, forming a protective layer. The seasoning is what keeps your food from sticking to the pan and protects the cast iron from rusting.

How to season

Before you season your cast iron pan, wash it well and make sure it is completely dry. You can place it on low heat in the oven or on a burner for a few minutes to dry it completely. Next, add a thin layer of oil to the pan and rub it in with a paper towel. Place the pan upside down in a 400°F (200°C) oven for about an hour. If your pan is sticky or gummy, it needs more time in the oven. Turn off the heat and allow the pan to cool. Repeat these steps as many times as necessary until your pan has a black, glossy finish.

Cast iron cookware on the market today comes pre-seasoned, but you still have to maintain the seasoning and re-season your cookware if the seasoning becomes degraded or damaged.

Oil choice

Every cast iron afficionado has an opinion about the best fat to use for seasoning. Some people swear by vegetable shortening, others prefer vegetable oil, and still others prefer bacon grease. There are seasoning sprays available as well. Keep in mind when choosing your oil how much use your cookware gets. If you don't use your pan often, the oil you use to season it can go rancid. Food cooked in a rancid-smelling skillet or Dutch oven will take on a rancid flavour. We have found canola oil works well in our recipes because it has a relatively high smoke point and does not go rancid quickly.

Cleaning

To keep your cast iron in peak condition, wash it by hand with a little mild dish soap as soon as possible after you have finished cooking, preferably while it is still warm. To remove cooked-on food, sprinkle salt into the pan and scrub gently with a soft-bristled brush, a silicone scrubber or another non-abrasive scrubber (bunched-up aluminum foil works, too). You can buy special chainmail scrubbers that do a wonderful job of removing caked-on food without damaging the seasoning, but food debris can be difficult to clean out of the scrubber.

Once the pan is clean, dry it thoroughly with a lint-free cloth or paper towel. You can warm the cookware on a burner or in the oven on low for a few minutes to make sure it is completely dry. Add a bit of oil and rub it in with paper towel. When you are done, your pan should be dry, not oily or sticky to the touch.

Storage

If you won't be using your cast iron cookware for a while, proper storage is essential. Keep the pan or Dutch oven in a place where it will be protected from moisture and dust. Do not store a Dutch oven with the lid on or the seasoning could go rancid, or moisture can build up inside and the oven can rust. You want the air to circulate around the pot, so put a spacer, such as a few sheets of paper towel rolled up, between the lid and the base to allow air flow.

Do's and Don'ts

Use this handy list of do's and don'ts to keep your cast iron cookware in peak condition.

Do preheat because of its relatively low thermal conductivity, cast iron takes longer to heat up, and as it does, the heat is not distributed evenly. For best results and to avoid hot spots, give your pan time to heat thoroughly before adding your food.

Do dry it thoroughly and rub with it oil after every use. This will help maintain the seasoning and prevent your pan from rusting

Do watch out for your hands. Cast iron retains heat, so the handles will be hot to the touch for a long time after you remove it from the heat source. Use a potholder, oven mitt or silicone holder when grabbing a handle or moving the pan around.

Don't add cold water to a hot pan or dip a hot pan into cold water. The sudden change in temperature could cause the cast iron to crack

Don't soak cast iron. You could destroy the seasoning and make the pan vulnerable to rust

Don't use harsh cleaners or abrasive scrubbers such as wire brushes or steel wool to clean your cookware (see Cleaning, above).

Don't let it drip dry or put away a pan that hasn't been dried thoroughly. The longer cast iron remains wet, the more prone it is to rust

Don't put your cast iron cookware in the dishwasher. You will destroy the seasoning

Do not store food in your cast iron cookware, especially if it is acidic. If food sits in a cold pan, the moisture will cause the pan to rust.

Enameled Cast Iron

Enameled cast iron is simply cast iron cookware that has been coated with a protective layer of enamel. Enameled cast iron comes in many different shapes and colours. It is a little easier to care for than traditional cast iron because it doesn't need to be seasoned and it is much easier to clean. However, this convenience comes with a price, namely less durability. The enamel layer can chip, scratch and if you knock the pan too hard or drop it, the enamel can even crack. Protect your enameled cookware by using silicone or wooden utensils instead of metal.

Mythbusting

A lot of misinformation exists about cast iron. Below we dispel a few of the most common myths.

Myth: You can't cook acidic foods, such as tomatoes.

Not true! If your pan is well-seasoned, cooking acidic foods such as tomato-based dishes isn't a problem, though you shouldn't leave them in the pan for too long. Avoid acidic dishes with long simmering times, or use enameled cast iron instead.

Myth: You can't use dishwashing liquid to clean cast iron.

Wrong! Washing your cast iron with mild dish soap is perfectly safe. Avoid harsh chemicals, though, that could damage your seasoning.

Myth: You can't use cast iron on glass stovetops.

Wrong again. Cast iron works wonderfully on glass stovetops, although be careful not to scratch the stovetop with your heavy cast iron pan. Make sure you place your pan carefully on the stovetop, and lift it up to move it instead of sliding it.

Induction stovetops, which use an electromagnetic field under a glass layer to transfer energy to the cookware, work great with cast iron because the iron draws out the electromagnetic current. This allows the cast iron pan or pot to heat faster than on a gas or electric stovetop.

Myth: A rusty cast iron pot or pan is garbage.

Nope! If you see rust on your cast iron, scrub it off and re-season the pan, repeating the steps as many times as it takes to rebuild that shiny black patina.

Blueberry Pancakes

Pancakes are a great way to start off any day, especially while camping! Cooking them over the campfire is a great way to enjoy a rustic outdoor experience. If your pancakes are browning too quickly, raise the grill a little higher away from the coals.

All-purpose flour	1 cup	250 mL
Baking powder	1 tsp.	5 mL
Baking soda	1/2 tsp.	2 mL
Milk	1 cup	250 mL
Large egg, fork-beaten	1	1
Melted butter	2 tbsp.	30 mL
Blueberries	1 cup	250 mL
Butter (or hard margarine)	1 tbsp.	15 mL

Prepare campfire for cooking. Combine flour, baking powder and baking soda in a medium bowl. Mix well.

In a separate bowl, combine milk, egg and butter. Pour into dry ingredients and stir until just moistened. Add blueberries, stirring until just combined. Batter will be lumpy.

Heat a large cast iron skillet to medium on a grill 2 to 3 inches (5 to 7.5 cm) above hot coals of campfire. Add butter. Once butter has melted, add 1/4 cup (60 mL) batter. Cook until deep holes or bubbles appear in pancake. Flip pancake over and cook other side until golden brown. Repeat for each pancake. Makes about 12 pancakes.

1 pancake: 90 Calories; 3.5 g Total Fat (1 g Mono, 0 g Poly, 2 g Sat); 25 mg Cholesterol; 11 g Carbohydrate (0 g Fibre, 2 g Sugar); 3 g Protein; 115 mg Sodium

Mushroom and Asparagus Frittata

A well-seasoned cast iron skillet is the perfect utensil for cooking frittatas over your campfire. You need to add a lot of extra fat to a stainless-steel skillet to prevent the eggs from sticking, but with a properly seasoned cast iron skillet, your frittata will slide right out!

Large eggs	8	8
Heavy cream	1/4 cup	60 mL
Grated Cheddar cheese	2 tbsp.	30 mL
Cooking oil	2 tbsp.	30 mL
Chopped onion	1/2 cup	125 mL
Thinly sliced mushrooms	1 cup .	250 mL
Asparagus, thin spears	1 cup	250 mL
cut into 2 inch (5 cm) pieces		
Chopped fresh basil	3 tbsp.	45 mL
Salt	1/2 tsp.	2 mL
Pepper	1/2 tsp.	2 mL
Halved cherry tomatoes	3/4 cup	175 mL
Grated Cheddar cheese	3 tbsp.	45 mL

Prepare campfire for cooking. Whisk together eggs, cream and first amount of cheese in a medium bowl. Set aside.

Heat a 12 inch (30 cm) cast iron skillet to medium on a grate 2 to 3 inches (5 to 7.5 cm) above hot coals of campfire. Add oil. Add onion and cook, stirring often, until softened, about 5 minutes. Add mushrooms and cook, stirring often, until soft and all liquid has evaporated, about 5 to 6 minutes. Add asparagus, basil, salt and pepper and cook, stirring often, for 2 to 3 minutes.

Pour egg mixture over mushroom mixture and cook for 8 to 12 minutes until eggs have started to set. Sprinkle with cherry tomatoes and second amount of cheese. Cook until eggs are set completely and cheese has melted, about 3 to 6 minutes. Slice and serve. Makes 6 servings.

1 serving: 340 Calories; 27 g Total Fat (10 g Mono, 2.5 g Poly, 12 g Sat); 330 mg Cholesterol; 5 g Carbohydrate (1 g Fibre, 2 g Sugar); 20 g Protein; 550 mg Sodium

Cowboy's Breakfast

Loaded with bacon, potato, green pepper and two kinds of cheese, this skillet is a one-stop breakfast dish!

Bacon slices, diced	6	6
Chopped green onion	1/4 cup	60 mL
Chopped onion	1/4 cup	60 mL
Frozen hash brown potatoes, thawed	2 cups	500 mL
Large eggs	4	4
Water	1/4 cup	60 mL
Salt	1/2 tsp.	2 mL
Pepper	1/8 tsp.	0.5 mL
Grated medium Cheddar cheese	1/2 cup	125 mL
Grated part-skimmed mozzarella cheese	1/2 cup	125 mL
Sliced green onions	2 tbsp.	30 mL

Prepare campfire for cooking. Heat a 12 inch (30 cm) cast iron skillet to medium on a grate 2 to 3 inches (5 to 7.5 cm) over hot coals of campfire. Add first 3 ingredients and cook, stirring often, for 5 to 10 minutes until bacon is crisp. Transfer with a slotted spoon to a plate lined with paper towel to drain. Drain and discard all but 1 tbsp. (15 mL) drippings from skillet.

Add hash browns to same skillet. Cook for about 7 to 10 minutes, stirring occasionally, until crisp.

Beat next 4 ingredients in a small bowl. Stir in bacon mixture and pour over hash browns.

Sprinkle with half of Cheddar and mozzarella. Cook for about 5 to 7 minutes, stirring occasionally, until almost set. Sprinkle with remaining cheese. Cover with a lid and cook for another 2 or 3 minutes until cheeses are melted. Garnish with green onions. Makes 4 servings.

1 serving: 590 Calories; 46 g Total Fat (19 g Mono, 4.5 g Poly, 18 g Sat); 275 mg Cholesterol; 24 g Carbohydrate (2 g Fibre, 2 g Sugar); 21 g Protein; 1040 mg Sodium

Butter-basted Rib-eye Steak

This is a steak you want to have only occasionally—it's a cardiologist's nightmare, but a steak lover's dream. It is rich, meaty and well caramelized on the outside—and it melts in your mouth. As with the other cast iron skillet recipes in this book, the key is to get the pan scorching hot. We've cooked it outside on a barbecue because of how much the steak smokes when it hits the pan, but you could also cook it indoors on your stovetop, if you prefer. Season the meat well and do not overcook it—anything past medium may be too much.

Thick rib-eye or prime rib steak	2 lbs.	900 g
Cooking oil	1 tbsp.	15 mL
Kosher salt	1 tbsp.	15 mL
Cold butter	1/4 cup	60 mL
Pepper	1 tbsp.	15 mL

If steak has been refrigerated, allow it to come to room temperature. Rub with oil and season with salt on all sides.

Heat a 12 inch (30 cm) cast iron skillet on side burner or grill of a barbecue for about 15 minutes until very hot. Add steak; there should be lots of smoke. Press steak down so entire surface makes contact with pan. Cook for 7 to 10 minutes depending on thickness of meat. Flip steak and add butter to pan. Cook for 5 minutes, basting steak with butter every minute or so. Turn heat to low and cook, continuing to baste with butter, for another 5 minutes, or until it reaches desired doneness (see Tip, below). Season with pepper. Let stand for 5 to 7 minutes before serving. Makes 4 servings.

Tip: An instant-read thermometer takes the guesswork out of doneness in this recipe. Cook the steak until the internal temperature reaches 135° to 145°F (57° to 63°C) for medium.

1 serving: 720 Calories; 61 g Total Fat (5 g Mono, 1.5 g Poly, 26 g Sat); 210 mg Cholesterol; 1 g Carbohydrate (0 g Fibre, 0 g Sugar); 42 g Protein; 1790 mg Sodium

Campfire Chili

You can't go wrong with chili, a family favourite any time of the year. This dish is great for a family cookout but can also be made indoors on the stovetop, if rustic cooking is not your style.

Lean ground beef	1 1/2 lbs.	680 g
Chopped onion	1 1/2 cups	375 mL
Chopped red pepper	1 cup	250 mL
Garlic cloves, minced (or 1/2 tsp., 2 mL, powder)	2	2
Chunky salsa	3 cups	750 mL
Can of diced green chilies (4 oz., 113 mL)	1	1
Chili powder	1 tbsp.	15 mL
Ground cumin	1 tsp.	5 mL
Cans of red kidney beans (14 oz., 398 mL) rinsed and drained	2	2
Can of kernel corn (14 oz., 398 mL) rinsed and drained	1	1

Prepare campfire for cooking. In a cast iron Dutch oven, on a grate about 2 inches (5 cm) above hot coals, cook ground beef, onion and red pepper until beef is nicely browned, about 10 to 12 minutes. Drain off fat.

Add garlic. Cook, stirring constantly, until fragrant, about 2 minutes. Stir in salsa, chilies, chili powder and cumin. Stir in kidney beans and corn. Bring to a boil. Move Dutch oven farther away from coals to reduce heat to low. Cook, covered, for about 30 minutes, stirring occasionally, to blend flavours. Makes 8 servings.

1 serving: 390 Calories; 13 g Total Fat (5 g Mono, 0.5 g Poly, 4.5 g Sat); 50 mg Cholesterol; 40 g Carbohydrate (9 g Fibre, 13 g Sugar); 24 g Protein; 1220 mg Sodium

Brick Chicken

Bricks might seem like an odd kitchen accessory, but using them to press the chicken down on the cast iron skillet as it cooks makes the skin deliciously crispy.

Bricks	2	2
Butter	1/4 cup	60 mL
Fresh chopped thyme	2 tbsp.	30 mL
Lemon juice	2 tbsp.	30 mL
Garlic cloves, minced	2	2
(or 1/2 tsp., 2 mL, garlic powder)		
Lemon zest (see Tip, page 60)	1 tsp.	5 mL
Salt	1/2 tsp.	2 mL
Pepper	1/2 tsp.	2 mL
Whole chicken	4 lbs.	1.8 kg
Olive oil	3 tbsp.	45 mL

Prepare campfire for cooking. Wrap bricks with foil and set aside.

Combine first 7 ingredients in a small bowl. Set aside.

Place chicken, backbone up, on a cutting board. Using kitchen shears or a sharp knife, cut down both sides of backbone to remove. Turn chicken over and press flat. Carefully loosen but do not remove chicken skin. Stuff lemon butter between meat and skin, and spread mixture as evenly as possible.

Secure opening with wooden toothpicks. Brush chicken with oil. Preheat a deep 12 inch (30 cm) cast iron skillet to medium on a grate 2 to 3 inches (5 to 7.5 cm) above hot coals of campfire. Place chicken in skillet breast side down. Place bricks directly on chicken to flatten. Cook for about 12 minutes, until skin is crispy. Remove bricks and carefully turn chicken over. Place bricks back on and cover with foil. Cook for 20 minutes. Remove foil and bricks and flip chicken over again so skin side is down. Replace bricks and cook until internal temperature reaches 165°F (75°C), about 5 to 10 minutes. Remove bricks from chicken and transfer chicken to a platter. Set aside to rest for 5 to 10 minutes before carving. Makes 6 servings.

1 serving: 700 Calories; 54 g Total Fat (23 g Mono, 10 g Poly, 17 g Sat); 220 mg Cholesterol; 0 g Carbohydrate (0 g Fibre, 0 g Sugar); 49 g Protein; 240 mg Sodium

Caramelized Cast Iron Scallops with Drambuie Butter

This recipe is perfect for your portable camp stove, but it can also be prepared on the side burner of a barbecue. It makes a great appetizer at any outdoor gathering. These scallops are quite large, which is what you want for this recipe. The numbers "10/20" mean that there are roughly 10 to 20 scallops per pound.

10/20 scallops	2 lbs.	900 g
Cooking oil	2 tbsp.	30 mL
Butter	1/4 cup	60 mL
Drambuie or Scotch	1 tbsp.	15 mL
Maple syrup	1 tbsp.	15 mL
Salt	2 tsp.	10 mL
Pepper	1 tsp.	5 mL

Heat a 12 inch (30 cm) cast iron skillet on side burner or grill of a barbecue for 10 to 15 minutes to medium. Dry scallops well so there is no moisture on them.

Pour oil onto a plate. Dip both flat surfaces of each scallop in oil, making sure to cover each one evenly. Place half of scallops flat side down in hot skillet and gently push down with a spatula so they are flat against pan. Cook for 2 to 3 minutes, just until first side is caramelized. Flip and cook other side for 1 minute, until scallops are caramelized on top and opaque throughout. Transfer to a warm plate. Repeat with remaining scallops.

Add butter, Drambuie and maple syrup to pan and cook, stirring, until butter has melted. Season with salt and pepper. Remove skillet from heat and add scallops, turning gently to coat with sauce. Serve immediately. Makes 8 servings as an appetizer.

1 serving: 190 Calories; 10 g Total Fat (3.5 g Mono, 1.5 g Poly, 4 g Sat); 55 mg Cholesterol; 4 g Carbohydrate (0 g Fibre, 1 g Sugar); 19 g Protein; 810 mg Sodium

Cast Iron Mussels

Dining al fresco is truly one of life's simple pleasures. There is something about eating outside in the fresh air that just makes food taste better. In this dish, the flavour of the mussels really comes out because they are not immersed in a broth. As the mussels start to cook, their juices hit the skillet and infuse the mussles with the smokiness of their own sizzling hot liquid. Serve with a loaf of fresh bread and a great white wine.

Olive oil	1/4 cup	60 mL
Garlic cloves, minced	6	6
(or 1 1/2 tsp., 7 mL, powder)		
Chopped fresh chives	2 tbsp.	30 mL
Mussels, cleaned and debearded	3 lbs.	1.4 kg
(see Tip, below)		
Salt, to taste		
Pepper, to taste		

Combine oil, garlic and chives in a small bowl. Set aside.

Heat a 12 inch (30 cm) cast iron skillet on side burner or grill of a barbecue over high heat for 15 minutes. Add mussels. Cook until mussels have steamed open, about 6 to 7 minutes. Pour oil mixture over mussels and season with salt and pepper. Makes 6 servings.

1 serving: 260 Calories; 14 g Total Fat (8 g Mono, 2.5 g Poly, 2 g Sat); 85 mg Cholesterol; 9 g Carbohydrate (0 g Fibre, 0 g Sugar); 24 g Protein; 1320 mg Sodium

Tip: To debeard mussels, grasp the stringy bits using a dishcloth and gently pull them off.

Tequila Trout with Salsa Fresca

Tequila gives a nice little kick to both the freshly made salsa and the trout fillets. This dish would pair well with roasted potatoes and a crisp white wine.

Plum tomatoes, diced	6	6
Medium onion, diced	1	1
Jalapeño pepper, seeded and minced (see Tip, below)	1	1
Chopped fresh cilantro	2 tbsp.	30 mL
Lime juice	1 tbsp.	15 mL
Cumin powder	1 tbsp.	15 mL
Garlic powder	1 tbsp.	15 mL
Tequila	1 tbsp.	15 mL
Salt	1 tsp.	5 mL
Pepper	1 tsp.	5 mL
Cooking oil	2 tbsp.	30 mL
Trout fillets (6 oz., 170 g, each)	6	6
Chili powder	2 tsp.	10 mL
Lemon pepper	2 tsp.	10 mL
Dried dill weed	1 tsp.	5 mL
Tequila	6 tbsp.	90 mL
Chopped fresh cilantro, for garnish		

For the salsa, add first 10 ingredients to a food processor. Pulse briefly a few times for a chunky texture. Transfer to a bowl and set aside in a refrigerator or a cooler.

Prepare campfire for cooking. Heat a 14 inch (35 cm) cast iron skillet to medium-high on a grate 2 to 3 inches (5 to 7.5 cm) above hot coals. Add oil and heat until barely smoking. Sprinkle fillets with chili powder, lemon pepper and dill, and cook for 5 to 7 minutes, turning once, until fish is golden brown and flakes easily when tested with a fork.

Remove pan from heat and splash 1 tbsp. (15 mL) tequila on each fillet. Carefully ignite tequila with a match or lighter. Shake pan gently until flames subside. Transfer to individual plates. Top with salsa and garnish with cilantro. Makes 6 servings.

1 serving: 310 Calories; 11 g Total Fat (4.5 g Mono, 3.5 g Poly, 1.5 g Sat); 100 mg Cholesterol; 7 g Carbohydrate (2 g Fibre, 3 g Sugar); 36 g Protein; 570 mg Sodium

Tip: Hot peppers contain capsaicin in the seeds and ribs. Removing the seeds will reduce the heat. Wear rubber gloves when handling hot peppers and avoid touching your eyes. Wash your hands well afterwards.

Mushroom Ragout

This dish pairs perfectly with any grilled meat and for convenience can be cooked on the side burner of your barbecue as your meat is grilling. You can use any mushrooms in this recipe: oyster, chanterelles, shiitake, brown, button, etc. If you can get fresh wild mushrooms, that's great, but button mushrooms from any grocery will work as well. Sometimes grocery stores will stock wild mushrooms, or you can check out the local farmers' markets. Morels usually appear in markets in spring, and throughout the summer different varieties are available across the country. If you're out picking mushrooms yourself, make sure you have an authoritative identification guide with you—some species are poisonous.

Extra-virgin olive oil	2 tbsp.	30 mL
Dried crushed red chilis	1 tsp.	5 mL
Whole cloves garlic, peeled	3	3
Medium onion, sliced	1/2	1/2
Mushrooms	12 cups	3 L
Dry (or alcohol-free) white wine	1/2 cup	125 mL
Diced tomatoes	4	4
Balsamic vinegar	2 tbsp.	30 mL
Chopped fresh herbs (such as oregano, thyme, rosemary or a combination)	2 tbsp.	30 mL

Heat a deep 14 inch (35 cm) cast iron skillet on a grill or side burner of a barbecue to medium. Add oil. Add red chili flakes and cook until they begin to crackle, about 1 or 2 minutes. Add garlic and cook until fragrant, about 2 minutes. Add onion and cook for 3 to 5 minutes or until soft. Add mushrooms and cook for 3 to 5 minutes.

Add remaining 4 ingredients and turn heat to medium-low. Gently simmer, stirring occasionally, for up to 45 minutes, until almost all liquid is evaporated. Makes 6 servings.

1 serving: 100 Calories; 5 g Total Fat (3.5 g Mono, 0.5 g Poly, 1 g Sat); 0 mg Cholesterol; 9 g Carbohydrate (2 g Fibre, 5 g Sugar); 5 g Protein; 10 mg Sodium

Cast Iron Potatoes

This easy-to-prepare recipe is a perfect side dish for any grilled meat and cooks in a cast iron skillet on the grill of your barbecue alongside the meat you are grilling. The smoke from the grilling meat adds even more depth of flavour to the potatoes.

Baby potatoes, large ones cut in half	3 lbs.	1.4 kg
Extra-virgin olive oil	2 tbsp.	30 mL
Chopped fresh thyme	1 tbsp.	15 mL
Salt, to taste		
Pepper, to taste		

Place potatoes in a large cast iron skillet and add enough water to just cover potatoes. Place skillet on grill of barbecue heated to 450°F (230°C) and close lid. Cook until all water has evaporated, about 30 minutes.

Continue to cook potatoes in skillet, rolling them around so that their skins get crispy and just begin to break, about 10 to 15 minutes. Drizzle with oil and sprinkle with thyme. Season with salt and pepper. Makes 8 servings.

1 serving: 150 Calories; 3.5 g Total Fat (3 g Mono, 0 g Poly, 0 g Sat); 0 mg Cholesterol; 27 g Carbohydrate (4 g Fibre, 2 g Sugar); 3 g Protein; 10 mg Sodium

Bannock

Bannock is a kind of flatbread that can be cooked over a campfire by wrapping the dough around a tree branch or frying it in a greased skillet. We've cooked it in a cast iron skillet with perfectly crispy results. For a little variety, try adding a few raisins or berries to flavour the bannock, which has long been popular among First Nations and Inuit peoples as well as outdoorsmen and women throughout Canada. Basic bannock can also be made with boiled, mashed potatoes added to the dough.

All-purpose flour	2 cups	500 mL
Baking powder	1 tbsp.	15 mL
Butter (or hard margarine)	3 tbsp.	45 mL
Salt	1 tsp.	5 mL
Warm water	2/3 cup	150 mL
Cooking oil	1 tbsp.	15 mL

Place flour, baking powder, butter and salt in a large bowl and mix with your hands until dough clumps. Slowly add water and mix until dough softens (you may not use the entire 2/3 cup, 150 mL, water). Let dough rest, covered, for 30 minutes.

Prepare campfire for cooking. Divide dough into quarters and shape each portion into a ball. Flatten into a disk about 1/2 inch (1 cm) thick. Heat a skillet on a grate 2 to 3 inches (5 to 7.5 cm) above hot coals. Add oil. Cook bannock on both sides, turning once, until golden brown. Makes 4 servings.

1 serving: 340 Calories; 13 g Total Fat (4.5 g Mono, 1.5 g Poly, 6 g Sat); 25 mg Cholesterol; 48 g Carbohydrate (2 g Fibre, 0 g Sugar); 7 g Protein; 860 mg Sodium

Raspberry Cobbler

Although we have gone with raspberries in this dish, it would be equally delicious made with any fresh berries, especially blueberries, blackberries and even saskatoon berries, if you can find them.

All-purpose flour	1 cup	250 mL
Granulated sugar	1/2 cup	125 mL
Baking powder	1 tsp.	5 mL
Salt	1/2 tsp.	2 mL
Cold butter	6 tbsp.	90 mL
Boiling water	1/4 cup	60 mL
Cornstarch	2 tbsp.	30 mL
Cold water	1/4 cup	60 mL
Granulated sugar	1 cup	250 mL
Lemon juice	1 tbsp.	15 mL
Fresh raspberries	4 cups	1 L

Prepare campfire for cooking. In a large bowl, combine flour, first amount of sugar, baking powder and salt. Cut in butter until mixture resembles coarse crumbs. Stir in boiling water just until dough is evenly moist.

In a medium bowl, dissolve cornstarch in cold water. Mix in second amount of sugar, lemon juice and raspberries. Transfer mixture to a 10 inch (25 cm) cast iron skillet on a grate 2 to 3 inches (5 to 7.5 cm) above hot coals of campfire and bring to a boil, stirring frequently, until slightly thickened. Drop dough into skillet by the spoonful. Cook, covered, over coals for about 45 to 60 minutes, until bubbling and dough is golden brown. Makes 8 servings.

1 serving: 320 Calories; 9 g Total Fat (2.5 g Mono, 0.5 g Poly, 5 g Sat); 25 mg Cholesterol; 59 g Carbohydrate (4 g Fibre, 40 g Sugar); 2 g Protein; 240 mg Sodium

Corned Beef Hash and Eggs

This classic pairing of corned beef and potato is very tasty and thoroughly satisfying. This hearty dish will keep you going all morning long.

Diced cooked peeled potato (about 1/4 inch, 6 mm pieces)	2 cups	500 mL
Cooked corned beef, cut into chunks	1 lb.	454 g
Finely chopped onion	1/2 cup	125 mL
Milk	1 1/2 tbsp.	22 mL
Pepper	1/4 tsp.	1 mL
Butter (or hard margarine)	1 tbsp.	15 mL
Large eggs	4	4
Chopped fresh parsley	3 tbsp.	45 mL
Salt, to taste		

Combine first 5 ingredients in a medium bowl.

Heat a 12 inch (30 cm) cast iron skillet to medium. Add butter and heat until it melts. Stir in corned beef mixture. Cook, covered, for about 15 minutes, stirring occasionally, until heated through. Cook, uncovered, for about 35 minutes, stirring occasionally, until browned.

Make 4 holes in hash and break 1 egg into each. Cook, covered, for about 5 minutes or until eggs are cooked to desired doneness. Sprinkle with parsley and salt. Makes 4 servings.

1 serving: 390 Calories; 25 g Total Fat (11 g Mono, 1.5 g Poly, 9 g Sat); 280 mg Cholesterol; 16 g Carbohydrate (2 g Fibre, 2 g Sugar); 25 g Protein; 1480 mg Sodium

Shakshuka

Shakshuka is a classic dish that originated in North Africa and has since spread throughout much of the Middle East. It is a delicious one-dish meal that is full of warm spices and herbs. Although we've placed it in the breakfast section, it would be great for lunch or dinner as well.

Olive oil	2 tbsp.	30 mL
Chopped onion	2 cups	500 mL
Chopped green pepper	1 cup	250 mL
Garlic cloves, minced	3	3
Paprika	1 tsp.	5 mL
Ground cumin	1 tsp.	5 mL
Dried crushed red chilies	1/2 tsp.	2 mL
Salt	1/2 tsp.	2 mL
Pepper	1/4 tsp.	1 mL
Can of whole tomatoes (28 oz., 796 mL)	1	1
Tomato sauce	1/2 cup	125 mL
Large eggs	8	8
Chopped basil	1/4 cup	60 mL
Crumbled feta, optional	1/2 cup	125 mL

Heat a 12 inch (30 cm) cast iron skillet to medium. Add oil. Add onion and green peppers and cook, stirring constantly, until soft, about 8 to 10 minutes.

Add next 6 ingredients. Cook, stirring constantly, until fragrant, about 2 minutes. Reduce heat to medium-low.

Drain tomatoes, reserving liquid. Chop tomatoes into 4 pieces. Add tomatoes, reserved juices and tomato sauce to skillet. Cook, stirring occasionally, until reduced by half, about 8 or 9 minutes.

Make 8 depressions in sauce. Crack 1 egg into each depression. Cover pan and cook until eggs are set and yolk is soft, about 4 or 5 minutes. Remove from heat and garnish with basil and feta, if desired. Makes 8 servings.

1 serving: 180 Calories; 10 g Total Fat (4.5 g Mono, 1 g Poly, 3.5 g Sat); 220 mg Cholesterol; 11 g Carbohydrate (2 g Fibre, 6 g Sugar); 9 g Protein; 630 mg Sodium

Spanish Omelette

In Spain, this dish is served hot or cold, often as an appetizer. We like to serve this a weekday brunch dish, but because it is so simple and quick to prepare, you could also serve it as a weekday dinner paired with a garden salad.

Olive (or cooking) oil	1 tbsp.	15 mL
Peeled, cubed potatoes	2 cups	500 mL
Small onion, coarsely chopped	1	1
Large eggs	6	6
Water	3 tbsp.	45 mL
Seasoned salt	1/2 tsp.	2 mL
Pepper	1/4 tsp.	1 mL
Hot pepper sauce	1/4 tsp.	1 mL
Grated Monterey Jack cheese	3/4 cup	175 mL

Heat a 10 inch (25 cm) cast iron skillet to medium. Add oil. Add potato and onion and cook, stirring often, for about 20 minutes until onion is tender and potato has browned. Reduce heat to low.

Beat eggs, water, seasoned salt, pepper and hot pepper sauce in a medium bowl. Stir in cheese. Pour egg mixture into pan over potatoes. Cook, covered, on low for 8 minutes until bottom is browned. Place under broiler on top oven rack for 2 minutes until set and golden brown (see Tip, below). Cuts into 6 wedges.

1 wedge: 190 Calories; 11 g Total Fat (3.5 g Mono, 1 g Poly, 4.5 g Sat); 225 mg Cholesterol; 11 g Carbohydrate (0 g Fibre, 1 g Sugar); 10 g Protein; 300 mg Sodium

Tip: When baking or broiling food in a skillet with a handle that is not ovenproof, wrap the handle in foil and keep it to the front of the oven, away from the element.

Cherry Clafouti

A clafouti is usually served as a dessert, but we think it makes an excellent brunch dish. Though it is classically made with cherries, feel free to use whatever fruit is in season. Apples work great, as well as apricots and various berries. The world is your fruit basket.

Butter (or hard margarine), room temperature	2 tsp.	10 mL
Fresh sweet cherries, pitted and halved	2 1/2 cups	625 mL
Large eggs	3	3
Granulated sugar	1/2 cup	125 mL
Milk	1 1/4 cup	300 mL
Vanilla extract	1 tsp.	5 mL
Finely grated lemon zest	1 tsp.	5 mL
All-purpose flour	1 cup	250 mL
Salt	1/4 tsp.	1 mL
Granulated sugar	2 tbsp.	30 mL
Icing (confectioner's) sugar	1 tbsp.	15 mL

Rub butter inside a 12 inch (30 cm) cast iron skillet, covering bottom and sides. Scatter cherry halves on bottom of skillet. Set aside.

In a medium bowl, blend eggs and first amount of sugar until foamy. Add milk, vanilla and lemon zest. Blend well. Add flour and salt, and mix until just combined.

Pour batter over cherries and sprinkle with remaining sugar. Place skillet in 375°F (190°C) oven and bake for 30 to 35 minutes until it is browned and puffed up. Let cool slightly and sprinkle with icing sugar. Serve warm. Makes 8 servings.

1 serving: 200 Calories; 3 g Total Fat (1 g Mono, 0 g Poly, 1.5 g Sat); 85 mg Cholesterol; 37 g Carbohydrate (1 g Fibre, 24 g Sugar); 6 g Protein; 130 mg Sodium

Dutch Baby with Cranberry Orange Compote

Dutch babies were introduced in the early 1900s in a café in Seattle, Washington. They were based on German pancakes and were originally served as three small "babies" topped with icing sugar and a squeeze of lemon juice. Over time, the "Big Dutch baby" emerged, often served with fruit in the middle, and it is this variation that is most often seen in today.

Large orange	1	1
Cranberries (fresh or frozen, thawed)	1 1/2 cups	375 mL
Brown sugar, packed	1/2 cup	125 mL
Orange juice	1/4 cup	60 mL
Vanilla extract	1/2 tsp.	2 mL
Orange zest (see Tip, page 60)	1 tbsp.	30 mL
All-purpose flour	1/2 cup	125 mL
Salt	1/2 tsp.	2 mL
Large eggs	2	2
Milk	1/2 cup	125 mL
Butter (or hard margarine), melted	2 tbsp.	30 mL
Orange zest (see Tip, page 60)	2 tsp.	10 mL
Butter (or hard margarine)	1 tbsp.	15 mL
Icing (confectioner's) sugar, for dusting		

Segment orange and cut each segment into 3 pieces. Set aside.

In a medium saucepan, add half of cranberries, brown sugar and orange juice. Cook on medium heat until cranberries begin to break down, about 6 to 8 minutes. Add remaining cranberries, brown sugar and orange juice and cook for another 5 minutes, stirring occasionally. Stir in vanilla.

Remove from heat and add first amount of orange segments and orange zest, stirring until well combined. Cool to room temperature.

For the Dutch baby, combine flour and salt in a small bowl.

Blend eggs in a blender on low speed. Add flour mixture and milk, alternating in 6 additions. Blend until smooth. Add butter and remaining orange zest. Blend until smooth.

Heat a 9 inch (23 cm) cast iron skillet with second amount of butter on middle rack of a 450°F (230°C) oven. When butter is melted, carefully pour Dutch baby batter into skillet and bake for 25 minutes. Reduce heat to 350°F (175°C) and bake for 10 minutes.

Serve Dutch baby with compote and a dusting of icing sugar. Makes 4 servings.

1 serving: 330 Calories; 12 g Total Fat (3 g Mono, 1 g Poly, 6 g Sat); 130 mg Cholesterol; 52 g Carbohydrate (3 g Fibre, 33 g Sugar); 7 g Protein; 420 mg Sodium

Grilled Cheese Sandwich

One of the great things about cast iron cookware is that it distributes the heat evenly, which in this recipe means that the bread of this deliciously cheesy sandwich will be perfectly golden and crispy. Feel free to switch up the bread or cheeses if you are feeling adventurous. Sourdough bread would be amazing, or try adding a some jalapeño Monterey Jack cheese if you like things a little spicy.

Multigrain sandwich bread slices	4	4
Cheddar cheese slices	4	4
Swiss cheese slices	2	2
Mayonnaise	2 tbsp.	30 mL
Butter (or hard margarine)	2 tbsp.	30 mL

Place 2 slices of bread on a work surface. Arrange 2 slices of Cheddar cheese and 1 slice of Swiss cheese on each slice of bread. Top with remaining bread slices. Carefully spread mayonnaise on top and bottom surfaces of each sandwich.

Heat a 12 inch (30 cm) skillet to medium. Add 1 tbsp. (15 mL) butter and heat until it melts. Add first sandwich and cook until golden on one side, about 3 minutes. Flip over and cook, pressing down on sandwich, for 3 minutes. Remove sandwich from pan. Reheat pan if necessary and repeat with remaining butter and sandwich. Makes 2 servings.

1 serving: 690 Calories; 43 g Total Fat (10 g Mono, 6 g Poly, 20 g Sat); 95 mg Cholesterol; 47 g Carbohydrate (6 g Fibre, 4 g Sugar); 23 g Protein; 810 mg Sodium

Croque Monsieur

The croque monsieur originated in French cafés more than 100 years ago and has been a delicious crunchy, cheesy standard ever since. This is a dish that really benefits from being cooked in a cast iron skillet to ensure the sandwich gets a perfectly crispy exterior.

Butter (not margarine)	3 tbsp.	45 mL
All-purpose flour	3 tbsp.	45 mL
Warm milk	1 1/2 cup	375 mL
Salt	1/2 tsp.	2 mL
White pepper	1/2 tsp.	2 mL
Ground nutmeg	1/4 tsp.	1 mL
Grated Swiss cheese	1/2 cup	125 mL
Butter (or hard margarine)	2 tbsp.	30 mL
Brioche bread slices	8	8
Dijon mustard	2 tbsp.	30 mL
Thin deli ham slices	4	4
Grated Swiss cheese	2 cups	500 mL

For the Béchamel sauce, melt first amount of butter in a small pot on low. Add flour and whisk for 2 minutes. Slowly add warm milk, whisking constantly to prevent lumps. Bring to a boil and reduce to a simmer, stirring constantly.

Whisk in salt, white pepper and nutmeg. Cook for about 5 minutes, stirring occasionally. Remove from heat. Stir in Swiss cheese and set aside.

Heat a 12 inch (30 cm) cast iron skillet to medium. Add 1 tbsp. (15 mL) butter and heat until melted. Add 4 slices of bread and toast on first side, about 2 minutes. Flip over and toast for another 1 to 2 minutes on second side. Remove from pan. Repeat with remaining butter and bread.

Spread 4 slices of bread with equal amounts of Dijon mustard. Top with deli ham. Spread 2 tbsp. (30 mL) Béchamel over ham and sprinkle with 1/4 cup (60 mL) Swiss cheese. Top with another slice of bread. Arrange sandwiches in skillet. Top each sandwich with remaining Béchamel and cheese. Cook in 400°F (200°C) oven for about 5 to 6 minutes. Switch oven to broiler and broil on high for 3 to 4 minutes until golden and bubbly (see Tip, page 40). Remove from oven and serve immediately. Makes 4 sandwiches.

1 sandwich: 710 Calories; 38 g Total Fat (8 g Mono, 1 g Poly, 22 g Sat); 130 mg Cholesterol; 60 g Carbohydrate (1 g Fibre, 13 g Sugar); 32 g Protein; 1300 mg Sodium

Roasting Coffee Beans

What could be better than a steaming cup of coffee made from freshly ground coffee beans you've roasted yourself? Your trusty cast iron skillet does an amazing job of roasting coffee beans, either over a campfire or on the barbecue. We recommend roasting your beans outside because the process is very smoky.

The key to roasting coffee beans is to avoid overcrowding your pan. Once your skillet is nice and hot, add your beans to the pan, ensuring they have enough space to move around. As the beans roast, shake the skillet or stir them constantly to keep them moving.

As the internal temperature of the coffee beans rises, the beans will reach two temperature thresholds, known as first and second crack.

First crack: As the beans go from green to light brown, the water in the beans begins to evaporate and is released as steam. At this point, the beans expand slightly in size. When they reach about 385°F (196°C), the beans begin to crack. This is the light roast stage. Contrary to popular belief, light roast beans actually have more caffeine than their dark roast counterparts. For medium roast, remove your beans before the second crack.

Second crack: The beans become dark brown, and when they reach about 435°F (224°C) you will hear a second crack. After the second crack, the oils in the beans move to the surface, giving them a shiny appearance. Watch your beans closely at this point because even an extra 30 seconds of roasting time can change the flavour. If you roast them too long, they will dry out and may even catch fire. The beans will also continue to roast even after they have been removed from the heat source. Beans that have been roasted to the second crack have less acidity and more body.

The entire roasting process takes about 10 to 20 minutes, depending on how dark a roast you prefer. Allow your beans to cool completely before storing them in an airtight container.

Beef Fajitas

Fajitas are a natural choice for cooking in your cast iron skillet. The cast iron retains its heat and gives the beef a perfect sear, trapping in its flavour. Serve with your favourite tortillas, corn or flour, and some salsa and guacamole on the side.

Cornstarch	1 tbsp.	15 mL
Garlic cloves, minced	3	3
(or 3/4 tsp., 3 mL, powder)		
Chili powder	2 tsp.	10 mL
Salt	1 tsp.	5 mL
Paprika	1 tsp.	5 mL
Granulated sugar	1 tsp.	5 mL
Onion powder	1/2 tsp.	2 mL
Ground cumin	1/2 tsp.	2 mL
Cayenne pepper	1/4 tsp.	1 mL
Skirt or flank steak, cut into	2 lbs.	900 g
1 inch (2.5 cm) pieces		
Olive oil	1 tbsp.	15 mL
Olive oil	1 tbsp.	15 mL
Medium green pepper, sliced	1	1
Medium red pepper, sliced	1	1
Medium yellow onion, sliced	1	1
Butter (or hard margarine)	1 tbsp.	15 mL
Lime juice	1/4 cup	60 mL
Chopped fresh cilantro, optional	2 tbsp.	30 mL

Combine first 9 ingredients in a small bowl.

Place steak, first amount of oil and spice mixture in a large resealable freezer bag. Seal and shake bag to ensure meat is evenly coated. Marinate in refrigerator for about 30 minutes.

Heat a 12 inch (30 cm) cast iron skillet to medium. Add remaining oil. Add peppers and onion and cook, stirring occasionally, for 4 to 5 minutes, until softened. Transfer to a large plate and set aside.

Reheat cast iron skillet to medium. Add butter and heat until melted. Transfer steak to skillet in a single layer and discard marinade. Cook steak for 2 to 3 minutes without stirring. Flip steak over and cook for 2 to 3 minutes on other side until browned. Stir in pepper mixture. Add lime and cook, stirring and scraping brown bits from the bottom of pan, until liquid is evaporated. Remove from heat and garnish with cilantro. Makes 6 servings.

1 serving: 400 Calories; 27 g Total Fat (13 g Mono, 1.5 g Poly, 10 g Sat); 95 mg Cholesterol; 8 g Carbohydrate (2 g Fibre, 3 g Sugar); 31 g Protein; 510 mg Sodium

Skillet Lasagna

Ahh, lasagna…the ultimate comfort food. This lasagna is cooked on the stovetop in a fraction of the time that traditional lasagna takes in the oven. This dish is perfect for busy weeknights when the last thing you want to do in the evening is prepare a time-consuming meal.

Ricotta cheese	1 1/2 cups	375 mL
Salt	1/2 tsp.	2 mL
Dried oregano	1/2 tsp.	2 mL
Pepper	1/2 tsp.	2 mL
Olive oil	2 tsp.	10 mL
Diced onion	3/4 cup	175 mL
Lean ground beef	1 lb.	454 g
Garlic cloves, minced	3	3
(or 3/4 tsp., 3 mL, powder)		
Salt	1/2 tsp.	2 mL
Pepper	1/2 tsp.	2 mL
Oven ready lasagna noodles, broken into pieces	8	8
Can of crushed tomatoes (28 oz., 796 mL)	1	1
Prepared beef broth	3/4 cup	175 mL
Italian seasonings	2 tsp.	10 mL
Grated mozzarella cheese	1 cup	250 mL
Grated Parmesan cheese	1/2 cup	125 mL
Chopped oregano, optional	2 tsp.	10 mL

Combine first 4 ingredients in a small bowl and set aside.

Heat a 12 inch (30 cm) cast iron skillet to medium. Add oil. Add onion and cook until softened, about 4 to 5 minutes. Increase heat to medium-high. Add ground beef and scramble-fry until meat is cooked through, about 6 to 8 minutes, stirring occasionally. Stir in garlic, salt and pepper and cook until fragrant, about 2 minutes. Drain off any excess grease from skillet.

Scatter lasagna noodles over ground beef.

Combine next 3 ingredients in a medium bowl and pour over lasagna noodles, ensuring noodles are completely covered. Do not stir. Bring mixture to a simmer and reduce heat to medium-low. Cook, covered, for about 10 to 15 minutes until noodles are soft. Remove lid and carefully stir mixture. Cook, covered, for another 10 minutes, stirring occasionally to ensure noodles do not stick to bottom of skillet. Add up to another 1/2 cup (125 mL) of broth, if needed. Turn off heat.

Dab ricotta mixture on top of noodle mixture and let stand for 5 minutes, covered, to warm cheese. Carefully fold ricotta mixture into noodle mixture. Sprinkle with both remaining cheeses. Broil on center rack on high for 2 to 3 minutes, until cheese is golden and bubbly.

Sprinkle with oregano. Makes 8 servings.

1 serving: 360 Calories; 17 g Total Fat (6 g Mono, 0.5 g Poly, 8 g Sat); 60 mg Cholesterol; 24 g Carbohydrate (3 g Fibre, 6 g Sugar); 25 g Protein; 920 mg Sodium

Swedish Meatballs

This creamy dish, seasoned with warm spices such as allspice and nutmeg, will become a family favourite.

Lean ground beef	2 lbs.	900 g
Fresh bread crumbs	3/4 cups	175 mL
Milk	1/3 cup	75 mL
Finely chopped onions	1/4 cup	60 mL
Large eggs, fork-beaten	2	2
Garlic cloves, minced	3	3
(or 3/4 tsp., 3 mL, powder)		
Salt	1 tsp.	5 mL
Ground allspice	1/4 tsp.	1 mL
Ground nutmeg	1/4 tsp.	1 mL
Pepper	1/4 tsp.	1 mL
Butter (or hard margarine)	3 tbsp.	45 mL
Cooking oil	3 tbsp.	45 mL
Butter (or hard margarine)	6 tbsp.	90 mL
All-purpose flour	6 tbsp.	90 mL
Warm prepared beef broth	2 1/2 cups	625 mL
Warm heavy cream	1 1/2 cups	375 mL
Worcestershire sauce	1 tbsp.	15 mL
Dijon mustard	2 tsp.	10 mL
Salt	1 tsp.	5 mL
Pepper	1 tsp.	5 mL

Combine first 10 ingredients in a large bowl. Mix well. With slightly wet hands, shape mixture into 48 balls. Set aside on a baking sheet.

Heat a high-sided 12 inch (30 cm) cast iron skillet to medium. Add 1 tbsp. (15 mL) each of butter and oil. Once butter has melted, add 1/3 of meatballs and cook, turning them every 1 or 2 minutes, until all sides are browned, about 6 to 8 minutes. Transfer to a plate. Repeat in 2 batches with remaining meatballs, butter and oil.

For the gravy, reheat cast iron skillet to medium. Add remaining butter and heat until melted. Add flour and whisk together for about 2 minutes. Reduce heat to medium-low. Slowly add beef broth, whisking constantly to prevent lumps. Add warm cream, whisking constantly to prevent lumps.

Add next 4 ingredients and whisk until combined. Bring to a boil and reduce to a simmer. Cook for about 5 to 6 minutes until gravy thickens slightly. Add meatballs back to skillet and stir carefully. Bring to a simmer and cook, uncovered, for 10 minutes, stirring occasionally, until meatballs are cooked through. Makes 48 meatballs.

4 meatballs: 400 Calories; 29 g Total Fat (11 g Mono, 2 g Poly, 14 g Sat); 125 mg Cholesterol; 10 g Carbohydrate (0 g Fibre, 1 g Sugar); 18 g Protein; 740 mg Sodium

Shepherd's Pie

A cast iron skillet is the perfect vessel for shepherd's pie because you can prepare the meat and vegetables on the stovetop and then transfer the skillet to the oven to get that fluffy, golden potato topping. This dish is also great way to use up any leftover mashed potatoes you may have on hand.

Peeled russet potatoes, cut into 1 inch (2.5 cm) pieces	1 lb.	454 g
Warm milk	1/4 cup	60 mL
Butter (or hard margarine)	2 tbsp.	30 mL
Salt	1 tsp.	5 mL
Pepper	1/2 tsp.	2 mL
Large egg yolk, fork-beaten	1	1
Olive oil	1 tbsp.	15 mL
Chopped onion	1 cup	250 mL
Chopped carrot	1 cup	250 mL
Garlic cloves, minced (or 3/4 tsp., 3 mL, powder)	3	3
Lean ground beef	1 1/2 lbs.	680 g
All-purpose flour	1 tbsp.	15 mL
Salt	1/4 tsp.	1 mL
Pepper	1/4 tsp.	1 mL
Prepared beef broth	1/2 cup	125 mL
Tomato paste (see Tip, page 83)	1 tbsp.	15 mL
Worcestershire sauce	1 tsp.	5 mL
Prepared horseradish	1 tsp.	5 mL
Frozen peas, thawed	1 cup	250 mL
Frozen corn, thawed	1 cup	250 mL
Chopped fresh thyme	2 tbsp.	30 mL
Melted butter (or hard margarine)	2 tbsp.	30 mL
Chopped fresh thyme	2 tsp.	10 mL

Cook potatoes in boiling salted water in a large saucepan until tender. Drain. Add next 4 ingredients and mash until potatoes are smooth. Fold in egg yolks and stir until well combined. Cover and set aside.

Heat a 12 inch (30 cm) cast iron skillet to medium. Add oil. Add onion and carrots and cook until onion begins to soften, about 3 to 4 minutes. Add garlic and cook until fragrant, about 1 minute.

Add ground beef to skillet and scramble-fry for about 10 minutes, until beef is no longer pink. Stir in next 3 ingredients.

Slowly add beef broth, stirring constantly. Add next 3 ingredients and cook, stirring, for about 5 to 6 minutes, until boiling and thickened. Fold in next 3 ingredients. Scoop mashed potatoes onto meat filling, spreading almost but not quite to edge. Brush with melted butter. Cook in 400°F (200°C) oven for about 30 minutes, until heated through and potatoes are golden. Sprinkle with thyme. Makes 6 servings.

1 serving: 450 Calories; 27 g Total Fat (11 g Mono, 1 g Poly, 12 g Sat); 125 mg Cholesterol; 17 g Carbohydrate (3 g Fibre, 3 g Sugar); 26 g Protein; 740 mg Sodium

Grainy Mustard and Thyme Tenderloin

Searing this pork tenderloin in a hot cast iron skillet before cooking it in the oven locks in the meat's natural juices and flavour, resulting in a deliciously juicy and tender dish. The lemon, mustard and thyme marinade imparts a special flavour that everyone will love.

Lemon juice	3 tbsp.	45 mL
Grainy mustard	2 tbsp.	30 mL
Honey	1 tbsp.	15 mL
Olive oil	1 tbsp.	15 mL
Fresh chopped thyme	1 tbsp.	15 mL
Garlic cloves, minced	3	3
(or 3/4 tsp., 4 mL, powder)		
Dijon mustard	2 tsp.	10 mL
Lemon zest (see Tip, below)	1 tsp.	5 mL
Salt	1/2 tsp.	2 mL
Pepper	1/2 tsp.	2 mL
Pork tenderloins (1 lb., 454 g, each)	2	2
Olive oil	2 tbsp.	30 mL

Fresh thyme, for garnish

Combine first 10 ingredients in a small bowl. Transfer to a resealable freezer bag. Add pork, seal bag and shake to coat. Marinate in refrigerator for 2 to 3 hours. Remove from marinade and discard marinade.

Heat a 14 inch (35 cm) cast iron skillet to medium. Add oil. Add tenderloin and brown on all sides, about 2 to 3 minutes per side. Transfer skillet to 350°F (175°C) oven and cook uncovered, turning occasionally for about 25 to 35 minutes, until internal temperature of pork reaches 160°F (71°C). Cover with foil and let stand for 5 minutes.

Cut into slices and garnish with thyme. Makes 6 servings.

1 serving: 285 Calories; 15 g Total Fat (9 g Mono, 1.5 g Poly, 4 g Sat); 100 mg Cholesterol; 6 g Carbohydrate (0 g Fibre, 3 g Sugar); 31 g Protein; 360 mg Sodium

Tip: When a recipe calls for grated zest and juice, it's easier to grate the fruit first, then juice it. Be careful not to grate down to the pith (the white part of the peel), which is bitter and is best avoided.

White Wine-marinated Pork Chops

Whether you cook your chops in a skillet or on the grill, this special marinade will make them deliciously juicy. It also works well with pork tenderloin.

Cooking oil	1 1/2 cups	375 mL
Soy sauce	3/4 cup	175 mL
Dry (or alcohol-free) white wine	1/2 cup	125 mL
Lemon juice	1/3 cup	75 mL
Worcestershire sauce	1/4 cup	60 mL
Ground dry mustard	2 tbsp.	15 mL
Chopped fresh parsley	1 1/2 tbsp.	22 mL
Pepper	1 tbsp.	15 mL
Salt	2 tsp.	10 mL
Bone-in pork loin rib chops, about 2 1/2 lbs. (1.1 kg)	6	6
Cooking oil	2 tbsp.	30 mL
Cooking oil	1 tsp.	5 mL
Sliced shallots	1/4 cup	60 mL
Whole garlic cloves, peeled	6	6
Chopped fresh rosemary	2 tbsp.	30 mL
Dry (or alcohol-free) white wine	3 tbsp.	45 mL
White balsamic vinegar	1/4 cup	60 mL
Whole rosemary leaves, for garnish		

Combine first 5 ingredients in a medium bowl. Whisk until well blended. Add mustard, parsley, pepper and salt and whisk until smooth. Pour marinade into a resealable freezer bag and add chops. Seal bag and shake to coat chops. Marinate in refrigerator for 8 hours or overnight. Remove chops from marinade and set aside. Discard marinade.

Heat a large cast iron skillet to medium-high. Add second amount of oil. Cook chops, in 2 batches, for 4 to 5 minutes per side, until no longer pink inside. Transfer to a serving platter and cover to keep warm.

Add remaining oil to skillet. Add shallots and cook for about 2 minutes, stirring often, until soft. Add garlic and rosemary and cook for 2 minutes, until garlic begins to brown. Add wine and cook until almost evaporated, scraping brown bits from bottom and sides of pan. Add balsamic vinegar. Cook until reduced by half, about 5 minutes. Divide sauce among pork chops. Garnish with rosemary leaves. Makes 6 servings.

1 serving: 310 Calories; 20 g Total Fat (10 g Mono, 3 g Poly, 5 g Sat); 60 mg Cholesterol; 7 g Carbohydrate (0 g Fibre, 3 g Sugar); 23 g Protein; 1090 mg Sodium

Rosemary and Lemon Lamb Chops

Pan-seared to perfection, these lamb chops are tender and juicy, flavoured with garlic, lemon and rosemary. Serve with roasted or Greek potatoes and steamed green beans or asparagus.

Olive oil	3 tbsp.	45 mL
Chopped fresh rosemary	2 tbsp.	30 mL
Garlic cloves, minced	8	8
(or 2 tsp., 10 mL, powder)		
Lemon zest	2 tsp.	10 mL
Salt	1 tsp.	5 mL
Pepper	1/2 tsp.	2 mL
Lamb rib chops (1 1/4 inch, 3 cm, thick, each), trimmed of fat	8	8
Olive oil	1 tbsp.	15 mL
Whole garlic cloves, peeled and smashed	8	8

Combine first 6 ingredients in a small bowl. Spoon rosemary mixture evenly over both sides of lamb. Marinate, covered, in refrigerator for up to 2 hours.

Heat 12 inch (30 cm) cast iron skillet to medium. Add oil. Add lamb and whole garlic cloves. Cook until lamb is browned, about 3 or 4 minutes per side or until desired doneness. Let rest for 5 minutes before serving. Makes 8 rib chops.

1 rib chop: 140 Calories; 10 g Total Fat (6 g Mono, 1 g Poly, 2 g Sat); 35 mg Cholesterol; 2 g Carbohydrate (0 g Fibre, 0 g Sugar); 12 g Protein; 330 mg Sodium

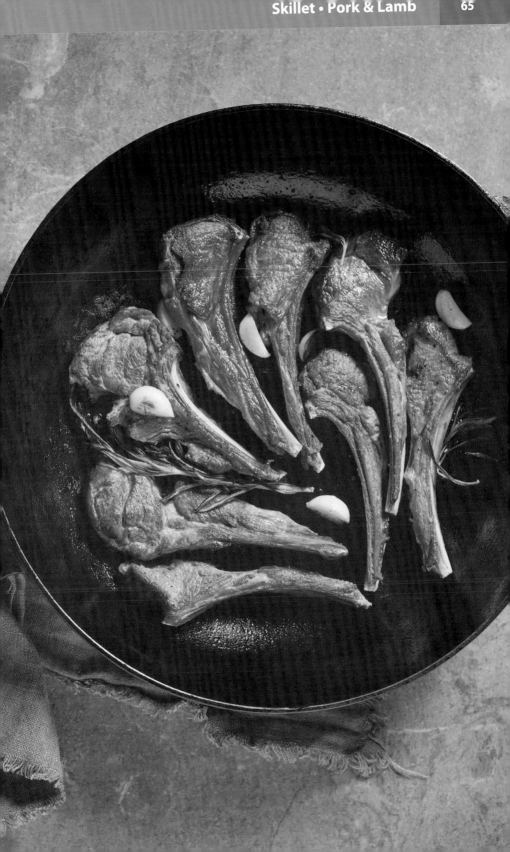

Chicken and Biscuits

Fluffy biscuits top a rich, creamy mixture of chicken, carrot, celery and mushrooms. The ultimate comfort food on a blustery fall or winter day.

All-purpose flour	1/2 cup	125 mL
Salt	1 tsp.	5 mL
Paprika	1/2 tsp.	2 ml
Pepper	1/2 tsp.	2 mL
Boneless, skinless chicken thighs, cut into 1 inch (2.5 cm) cubes	2 lbs.	900 g
Cooking oil	2 tbsp.	30 mL
Cooking oil	2 tbsp.	30 mL
Chopped onion	1 cup	250 mL
Chopped carrot	1 cup	250 mL
Sliced celery	1 cup	250 mL
Sliced mushrooms	1 cup	250 mL
Frozen peas, thawed	3/4 cup	175 mL
Garlic cloves, minced (or 1/2 tsp., 2 mL, powder)	2	2
All-purpose flour	1/4 cup	60 mL
Seasoned salt	1/2 tsp.	2 mL
Pepper	1/4 tsp.	1 mL
Warm milk	1 1/2 cups	375 mL
Warm prepared chicken broth	1 cup	250 mL
All-purpose flour	1 cup	250 mL
Baking powder	2 tsp.	10 mL
Salt	1/2 tsp.	2 mL
Milk	1/2 cup	125 mL
Large eggs	2	2

Combine first 4 ingredients in a large resealable freezer bag. Add chicken. Seal bag and toss to coat.

Heat a 12 inch (30 cm) cast iron skillet to medium. Add first amount of oil. Add half of chicken and cook until brown on all sides, about 6 to 8 minutes. Transfer to a plate and set aside. Repeat with remaining chicken.

Reheat skillet to medium. Add remaining oil. Add onion, carrot and celery and cook for 5 minutes, stirring occasionally. Add mushrooms and cook for 5 to 6 minutes, stirring occasionally, until onion and mushroom are softened. Stir in peas and garlic and cook until garlic is fragrant, about 2 minutes.

Reduce heat to low. Combine next 3 ingredients in a small bowl. Sprinkle over vegetables and cook, stirring constantly, for 2 minutes. Slowly whisk in milk. Whisk in chicken broth and bring to a simmer. Cook, stirring, until mixture thickens. Stir in chicken and cook for 5 minutes to allow flavours to combine.

Combine remaining flour, baking powder and salt in a medium bowl. Make a well in centre and add milk and eggs. Stir until just combined. Drop 8 spoonfuls of dough onto chicken mixture in skillet. Bake in 400°F (200°C) oven for 20 to 25 minutes, until golden and a wooden pick inserted in centre of biscuit comes out clean. Makes 8 servings.

1 serving: 350 Calories; 10 g Total Fat (4 g Mono, 2 g Poly, 2 g Sat); 150 mg Cholesterol; 32 g Carbohydrate (3 g Fibre, 7 g Sugar); 31 g Protein; 880 mg Sodium

Skillet Chicken Curry

This rich, enticing dish will be eagerly anticipated by friends and family alike.
Serve with hot basmati rice or naan to soak up every drop of decadent sauce.

Balkan-style yogurt	1 cup	250 mL
Lemon juice	2 tbsp.	30 mL
Garlic cloves, minced	4	4
(or 1 tsp., 5 mL, powder)		
Finely grated ginger root	2 tbsp.	30 mL
Curry powder	4 tsp.	20 mL
Smoked sweet paprika	4 tsp.	20 mL
Boneless, skinless chicken thighs,	2 lbs.	900 g
cut into 1 inch (2.5 cm) pieces		
Olive oil	2 tbsp.	30 mL
Ghee	2 tbsp.	30 mL
Cumin seed	2 tbsp.	30 mL
Finely chopped onion	2 cups	500 mL
Salt	1 tsp.	5 mL
Tomato paste (see Tip, page 83)	1/2 cup	125 mL
Prepared chicken broth	2 cups	500 mL
Whipping cream	1 cup	500 mL
Whole black cardamom pods	6	6
Bay leaves	4	4
Cinnamon sticks (4 inches, 10 cm, each)	2	2

Combine first 6 ingredients in a large resealable freezer bag. Add chicken and marinate in refrigerator for 4 hours. Drain and discard marinade. Heat a 12 inch (30 cm) cast iron skillet to medium. Add half of oil. Add half of chicken and sear until brown on all sides, about 3 or 4 minutes per side. Transfer to a plate. Repeat with remaining oil and chicken. Set aside.

Heat skillet to medium-high. Add ghee. Add cumin seed and cook, stirring constantly, for 30 seconds until toasted. Add onion and salt and reduce heat to medium. Cook for 7 minutes until onion is softened.

Add tomato paste and cook, stirring constantly, for 3 minutes until paste is slightly browned.

Add remaining 5 ingredients and stir until smooth. Bring to a boil and reduce heat to medium-low. Simmer for 10 minutes, stirring often, until sauce is thickened. Strain sauce through a sieve and return to pan. Discard solids. Add chicken to sauce and cook, stirring constantly, until heated through. Makes about 4 cups (1 L).

1/2 cup (125 mL): 310 Calories; 20 g Total Fat (6 g Mono, 2 g Poly, 9 g Sat); 125 mg Cholesterol; 8 g Carbohydrate (2 g Fibre, 4 g Sugar); 25 g Protein; 830 mg Sodium

Lemon Chicken Legs

This simple stovetop chicken is perfect for a weeknight dinner. The buttery, garlicky sauce is the perfect combination of sweet and sour, with a little heat thrown in from the chili sauce and crushed chilies. Serve over pasta or rice for a complete meal.

Olive oil	2 tbsp.	30 mL
Butter (or hard margarine)	1 tbsp.	15 mL
Finely chopped onion	1/4 cup	60 mL
Garlic cloves, minced	2	2
(or 1/2 tsp., 2 mL powder)		
Dried crushed red chilies	1/4 tsp.	1 mL
Lemon zest (see Tip, page 60)	1/4 tsp.	1 mL
Skinless chicken drumsticks	8	8
(about 4 oz., 113 g, each)		
Medium lemon, cut into 8 wedges	1	1
Prepared chicken broth	1/2 cup	125 mL
Brown sugar, lightly packed	1/4 cup	60 mL
Lemon juice	1/4 cup	60 mL
Thai sweet chili sauce	3 tbsp.	45 mL
Soy sauce	2 tbsp.	30 mL
Salt	1/2 tsp.	2 mL
Pepper	1/2 tsp.	2 mL
Butter (or hard margarine)	1 tbsp.	15 mL
Chopped fresh cilantro	1 tbsp.	15 mL
Sesame seeds	1 tsp.	5 mL

Heat a 14 inch (35 cm) cast iron skillet to medium. Add oil and first amount of butter. Add onion. Cook, stirring often, until onion is soft, about 3 minutes. Add garlic, red pepper flakes and lemon zest, cook, stirring often, until fragrant, about 2 minutes.

Add chicken and cook, stirring often, until browned on all sides, about 5 minutes. Add lemon wedges and cook for about 2 minutes.

Combine next 7 ingredients in a small bowl. Pour over chicken in skillet, scraping any brown bits from bottom of pan. Bring to a boil. Reduce heat to low and cook, covered, until drumsticks are cooked through, about 15 to 20 minutes.

Stir remaining butter into sauce. Garnish with cilantro and sesame seeds. Makes 8 drumsticks.

1 drumstick: 150 Calories; 8 g Total Fat (3.5 g Mono, 1 g Poly, 2.5 g Sat); 35 mg Cholesterol; 11 g Carbohydrate (0 g Fibre, 9 g Sugar); 8 g Protein; 510 mg Sodium

Chicken Piccata

Golden brown, breaded chicken breasts are nestled in a white wine sauce flavoured with lemon and capers. Serve this dish over a plate of your favourite type of noodle or a bed of basmati rice.

Boneless, skinless chicken breast (4 oz., 113 g, each)	4	4
Large eggs fork-beaten	2	2
Dry white (or alcohol-free) wine	2 tbsp.	30 mL
Lemon juice	2 tbsp.	30 mL
Garlic cloves, minced (or 3/4 tsp., 3 mL, powder)	3	3
All-purpose flour	1/2 cup	125 mL
Grated Parmesan cheese	1/2 cup	125 mL
Chopped parsley	2 tbsp.	30 mL
Salt	1 tsp.	5 mL
Pepper	1/2 tsp.	2 mL
Olive oil	2 tbsp.	30 mL
Dry (or alcohol-free) white wine	1/2 cup	125 mL
Prepared chicken broth	3/4 cup	175 mL
Garlic cloves, minced (or 1 tsp., 5 mL, powder)	4	4
Capers	2 tbsp.	30 mL
Lemon juice	1/4 cup	60 mL
Butter (or hard margarine)	2 tbsp.	30 mL
Chopped fresh parsley	2 tbsp.	30 mL

Place chicken breasts between 2 pieces of plastic wrap and pound with a mallet or rolling pin to 1/4 inch (6 mm) thickness.

Combine eggs, first amount of wine, lemon juice and garlic in a shallow dish.

Combine next 5 ingredients in a separate shallow dish. Coat chicken in flour mixture, then egg mixture and back into flour mixture. Transfer to a plate and set aside.

Heat a 12 inch (30 cm) cast iron skillet to medium-low. Add oil. Add chicken and cook until browned on both sides, about 6 or 7 minutes per side. Transfer to a plate and cover to keep warm.

Heat skillet to medium. Add remaining white wine, scraping up any brown bits from bottom of pan. Boil gently for 3 or 4 minutes, stirring occasionally, until about 1/4 cup (60 mL) liquid remains. Stir in broth, garlic, capers and remaining lemon juice. Bring to a simmer and cook for about 5 minutes, stirring occasionally, to allow flavours to combine and mixture to thicken slightly. Whisk in butter.

Return chicken to skillet and spoon sauce over top. Bring to a simmer and cook, covered, for 2 to 3 minutes until chicken is warmed through, whisking sauce if needed. Remove from heat and garnish with parsley. Makes 4 servings.

1 serving: 370 Calories; 13 g Total Fat (4 g Mono, 1 g Poly, 7 g Sat); 200 mg Cholesterol; 18 g Carbohydrate (0 g Fibre, 2 g Sugar); 36 g Protein; 1160 mg Sodium

Duck Breast with Berry Sauce

Duck fat is highly prized by chefs and foodies alike for its flavour, texture and versatility, so once you've rendered the fat from your duck breast, don't throw it out! Duck fat and potatoes are a perfect pairing, whether fried or roasted, resulting in potatoes with a deliciously golden, crispy crust. Duck fat also adds a real depth of flavour to roasted veggies, sauces, really anything you add it to, and is great for searing meat or rubbing on chicken before you roast it. It will keep for weeks in a sealed container in the fridge and can also be frozen if you want to store it longer.

Duck breast halves, fat trimmed (about 6 oz., 170 g, each)	4	4
Salt	1 tsp.	5 mL
Pepper	1 tsp.	5 mL
Cooking oil	1 tbsp.	15 mL
Finely chopped shallots	1/4 cup	60 mL
Dry (or alcohol-free) red wine	3/4 cup	175 mL
Chambord liqueur	3 tbsp.	45 mL
Cornstarch	1 tsp.	5 mL
Fresh (or frozen, thawed) raspberries	1/2 cup	125 mL
Fresh (or frozen, thawed) blueberries	1/4 cup	60 mL
Chopped fresh thyme	2 tbsp.	30 mL
Butter (or hard butter)	2 tbsp.	30 mL

With a fork, pierce duck through skin but not all the way to meat. Sprinkle with salt and pepper. Heat a 12 inch (30 cm) cast iron skillet to medium. Add oil. Add duck, skin side down, and cook for about 7 to 9 minutes until skin is brown and fat runs out. Remove skillet from heat and pour off fat. Return skillet to heat and cook duck, skin side up, for 7 to 9 minutes, or until desired doneness. Transfer to a plate, cover and set aside to rest. Remove all but 1 tbsp. (15 mL) of fat from pan.

Heat skillet to medium-low. Add shallots and cook, stirring constantly, for about 3 minutes until soft. Add wine and cook until reduced by half.

Combine Chambord and cornstarch. Whisk into wine sauce and simmer for about 3 minutes, whisking constantly, until thickened. Add raspberries, blueberries and thyme, and simmer for about 3 minutes, until berries are softened and heated through. Carefully mash berries with back of a fork. Run sauce through a sieve to remove any large pieces. Return sauce to skillet on low heat. Slowly whisk in butter. Remove from heat. Slice duck thinly and serve with sauce. Makes 4 servings.

1 serving: 570 Calories; 40 g Total Fat (18 g Mono, 5 g Poly, 14 g Sat); 150 mg Cholesterol; 6 g Carbohydrate (2 g Fibre, 2 g Sugar); 29 g Protein; 710 mg Sodium

Garlic Prawns

For best results, make sure you don't crowd the pan when cooking the prawns. If you overcrowd the pan, your prawns will stew instead of achieving that perfect sear you are looking for.

Butter (or hard margarine)	1/3 cup	75 mL
Garlic cloves, minced	4	4
(or 1 tsp., 5 mL, powder)		
Lemon juice	2 tbsp.	30 mL
Grainy mustard	2 tbsp.	30 mL
Finely chopped fresh rosemary	2 tbsp.	30 mL
Liquid honey	1 1/2 tbsp.	22 mL
Chili paste	1/2 tsp.	2 mL
Salt	1/4 tsp.	1 mL
Raw jumbo shrimp (prawns), shells left intact	16	16
Olive oil	1 tbsp.	15 mL

Melt butter in a medium saucepan on medium-low. Add garlic and cook, stirring, for 2 or 3 minutes, until softened. Remove from heat. Stir in next 6 ingredients.

Drizzle prawns with butter mixture.

Heat a 12 inch (30 cm) cast iron skillet to medium. Brush with oil. Add half of prawns and cook for about 5 minutes, turning once, until prawns are pink and curled. Transfer to a plate. Repeat with remaining prawns. Peel prawns and serve with remaining butter mixture. Makes 16 prawns.

1 prawn: 60 Calories; 4.5 g Total Fat (1.5 g Mono, 0 g Poly, 2.5 g Sat); 20 mg Cholesterol; 3 g Carbohydrate (0 g Fibre, 2 g Sugar); 3 g Protein; 120 mg Sodium

Spaghetti alle Vongole

Although this pasta dish is layered with the flavours of white wine, clams and garlic with a touch heat from the crushed chilies, it is the clams that really make the dish (vongole is Italian for "clams.") For best results, use the freshest clams you can find.

Little neck clams	2 lbs.	900 g
Water	8 cups	2 L
Salt	1 1/2 tsp.	7 mL
Spaghetti	8 oz.	225 g
Olive oil	3 tbsp.	45 mL
Chopped shallots	1/2 cup	125 mL
Garlic cloves, minced	4	4
(or 1 tsp., 5 mL, powder)		
Dried crushed red chilies	1/2 tsp.	2 mL
Dry (or alcohol-free) white wine	1 cup	250 mL
Chopped fresh parsley	1/4 cup	60 mL
Butter (or hard margarine)	2 tbsp.	30 mL
Grated Parmesan cheese	1/2 cup	125 mL
Chopped fresh parsley	2 tbsp.	30 mL
Lemon wedges, optional	4	4

Clean clams by soaking them in a large bowl of cold water for 30 minutes. Drain soaking water, replace with clean cold water and soak clams for 30 more minutes. Repeat steps until there is no sand and grit on bottom of bowl. Drain clams and set aside.

Combine water and salt in a Dutch oven and bring to a boil. Add pasta and cook, uncovered, for 9 to 11 minutes, stirring occasionally, until tender but firm. Drain, keeping 1/2 cup (125 mL) cooking liquid. Return pasta to same pot. Cover to keep warm.

Heat a 12 inch (30 cm) cast iron skillet to medium. Add oil. Add shallots and cook, stirring occasionally, until softened, about 4 to 5 minutes. Add garlic and red pepper flakes. Cook, stirring often, until fragrant, about 2 minutes.

Turn heat to medium-low and add wine, clams and first amount of parsley. Cook, covered, for about 6 minutes. Remove cover and discard any clams that have not opened. Add pasta and butter and toss to combine. Add about 1/4 cup (60 mL) reserved pasta liquid and toss again. If sauce is still dry, add remaining pasta liquid and toss.

Garnish with 3 remaining ingredients. Makes 4 servings.

1 serving: 670 Calories; 23 g Total Fat (10 g Mono, 2.5 g Poly, 8 g Sat); 105 mg Cholesterol; 62 g Carbohydrate (2 g Fibre, 4 g Sugar); 44 g Protein; 370 mg Sodium

Citrus Soy-glazed Salmon

A cast iron skillet is often touted as the best utensil for cooking salmon fillets, and for good reason. When preheated to the proper temperature, the cast iron skillet gives the skin of the fish that sought-after crispiness while leaving the flesh buttery soft. In this dish, a squeeze of fresh lemon further enhances the fabulous flavours. Serve with a side of grilled asparagus and cherry tomatoes.

Grapefruit juice	1 cup	250 mL
Sake	1/2 cup	125 mL
Granulated sugar	1/4 cup	60 mL
Low-sodium soy sauce	1/4 cup	60 mL
Dried crushed red chilies	1/4 tsp.	1 mL
Cornstarch	2 tsp.	10 mL
Water	2 tbsp.	30 mL
Mirin	2 tbsp.	30 mL
Lime juice	1 tbsp.	15 mL
Olive oil	1 tbsp.	15 mL
Salmon fillets (about 4 oz., 113 g, each)	4	4
Grated lemon zest	1 tsp.	5 mL

Bring first 5 ingredients to a boil in a small saucepan on medium-high, stirring often. Boil, uncovered, for 8 minutes, stirring occasionally, until reduced by half.

Stir cornstarch into water until smooth and add to saucepan. Cook, stirring, for 10 minutes until thickened.

Stir in mirin and lime juice. Transfer 1/4 cup (60 mL) glaze to a small cup.

Heat a cast iron grill pan to medium-high. Brush with oil. Add fillets and cook for 2 to 3 minutes per side, brushing with glaze, until fish flakes easily when tested with a fork. Transfer to a serving plate.

Drizzle with reserved glaze and sprinkle with lemon zest. Makes 4 servings.

1 serving: 430 Calories; 12 g Total Fat (5 g Mono, 3.5 g Poly, 2 g Sat); 70 mg Cholesterol; 46 g Carbohydrate (0 g Fibre, 41 g Sugar); 28 g Protein; 670 mg Sodium

Spicy Shrimp Jambalaya

This is the perfect one-dish meal. Spicy sausage and rice with tomato and the "holy trinity" of Cajun and Creole cooking—onion, bell peppers and celery. Because it is easier to find, we've used Italian sausage in this recipe, but you could substitute andouille sausage for a more authentic Creole flavour.

Cooking oil	1 tbsp.	15 mL
Sliced celery	1 cup	250 mL
Chopped green pepper	1 cup	250 mL
Chopped onion	1 cup	250 mL
Chopped red pepper	1/2 cup	125 mL
Sliced hot Italian sausage, casing removed	1/2 lb.	225 g
Can of diced tomatoes (28 oz., 796 mL), with juice	1	1
Prepared chicken broth	1 1/4 cups	300 mL
Tomato paste (see Tip, page 83)	3 tbsp.	45 mL
Hot pepper sauce	2 tsp.	10 mL
Garlic cloves, minced (or 1/2 tsp., 2 mL, powder)	2	2
Dried thyme	1 tsp.	5 mL
Granulated sugar	1/2 tsp.	2 mL
Cayenne pepper	1/4 tsp.	1 mL
Long grain white rice	3/4 cup	175 mL
Bay leaves	2	2
Uncooked medium shrimp, thawed, peeled and deveined	1 lb.	450 g
Chopped fresh parsley	2 tbsp.	30 mL

Heat a 12 inch (30 cm) cast iron skillet to medium. Add oil. Add next 5 ingredients and cook, stirring often, for about 8 minutes until sausage is no longer pink.

Add next 8 ingredients. Cook, stirring and scraping any brown bits from bottom of pan, until boiling. Stir in rice and bay leaves and bring to a boil. Reduce heat to medium-low. Simmer, covered, without stirring for 25 to 30 minutes until rice is tender. Discard bay leaves.

Add shrimp and stir gently. Cook, covered, for about 10 minutes until shrimp is pink and cooked through. Makes about 10 cups (2.5 L).

1 cup (250 mL): 220 Calories; 9 g Total Fat (4 g Mono, 1.5 g Poly, 3 g Sat); 85 mg Cholesterol; 20 g Carbohydrate (2 g Fibre, 5 g Sugar); 15 g Protein; 580 mg Sodium

Tip: If a recipe calls for less than an entire can of tomato paste, freeze the unopened can for 30 minutes. Open both ends and push the contents through one end. Slice off only what you need. Freeze the remaining paste in a resealable freezer bag or plastic wrap for future use.

Mac and Cheese

Thanks to the cast iron skillet, this mac and cheese is crispy on the bottom and sides, beautifully browned on top and gooey in the centre.

Water	8 cups	2 L
Salt	1 1/2 tsp.	7 mL
Elbow macaroni	8 oz.	225 g
Butter (or hard margarine)	1/4 cup	60 mL
All-purpose flour	1/4 cup	60 mL
Warm milk	3 cups	750 mL
Salt	1 tsp.	5 mL
Pepper	1/2 tsp.	2 mL
Ground nutmeg	1/2 tsp.	2 mL
Dry mustard	1/4 tsp.	1 mL
Grated Gruyere cheese	2 cup	500 mL
Grated Cheddar cheese	1 cup	250 mL
Grated Gouda cheese	1 cup	250 mL
Butter (or hard margarine), melted	3 tbsp.	45 mL
Bread crumbs	1 cup	250 mL

Combine water and salt in a Dutch oven and bring to a boil. Add pasta and cook, uncovered, for 7 to 9 minutes, stirring occasionally, until tender but still firm. Drain and return pasta to same pot, covering to keep warm.

Heat a 12 inch (30 cm) cast iron skillet to medium-low. Add butter and heat until melted. Add flour and cook, stirring constantly, for 1 minute. Turn heat to low. Slowly add milk, whisking constantly. Continue to whisk until boiling and thickened. Whisk in salt, pepper, nutmeg and dry mustard. Remove skillet from heat.

Combine cheeses in a medium bowl. Remove 1/2 cup (125 mL) cheese mixture and set aside. Slowly add remaining cheeses to skillet, stirring constantly until melted. Add macaroni and stir to coat.

Combine melted butter, bread crumbs and reserved cheese in a small bowl and sprinkle over macaroni mixture. Bake, uncovered, in 375°F (190°C) oven for about 20 minutes, until golden brown and bubbly. Makes 6 servings.

1 serving: 700 Calories; 39 g Total Fat (10 g Mono, 1.5 g Poly, 24 g Sat); 120 mg Cholesterol; 55 g Carbohydrate (2 g Fibre, 10 g Sugar); 34 g Protein; 1180 mg Sodium

Vegetarian Cast Iron Pizza

Cooking this pizza in a cast iron pan gives the homemade crust a perfect texture—nice and crispy on the bottom and sides but still light and a little puffy on the inside.

Warm water	3/4 cup	175 mL
Granulated sugar	1/2 tsp.	2 mL
Active dry yeast	2 tsp.	10 mL
All-purpose flour	2 cups	500 mL
Salt	1 1/2 tsp.	7 mL
Olive oil	2 tbsp.	30 mL
Pizza sauce	1/2 cup	125 mL
Thinly sliced fresh mushrooms	1 cup	250 mL
Chopped spinach	1/2 cup	125 mL
Chopped onions	1/2 cup	125 mL
Chopped yellow pepper	1/2 cup	125 mL
Dried oregano	1 tsp.	5 mL
Grated mozzarella cheese	1 cup	250 mL

For the crust, stir warm water and sugar in a small bowl until sugar is dissolved. Sprinkle yeast over top and let stand for 10 minutes. Stir until yeast is dissolved.

Combine flour and salt in a large bowl. Add yeast mixture and oil. Mix until dough pulls away from sides of bowl and is no longer sticky, adding a little more flour if necessary. Turn dough out onto a lightly floured surface. Knead for 5 to 10 minutes until smooth and elastic. Place in a large greased bowl, turning once to grease top. Cover with greased plastic wrap and a tea towel. Let stand in oven with light on and door closed for about 1 hour until doubled in size. Turn dough out onto a lightly floured surface and shape into a ball. Let stand for 20 minutes.

Heat a well-seasoned 12 inch (30 cm) cast iron skillet in 450°F (230°C) oven for 20 minutes. Remove from oven. Stretch dough out and fit into bottom of skillet. Spread evenly with pizza sauce. Layer next 4 ingredients over sauce. Sprinkle with dried oregano. Sprinkle with mozzarella cheese. Bake for 16 to 18 minutes, or until cheese is bubbly and crust is golden brown. Let pizza rest for 5 minutes before slicing. Cuts into 8 wedges.

1 wedge: 180 Calories; 4.5 g Total Fat (1.5 g Mono, 0 g Poly, 1.5 g Sat); 5 mg Cholesterol; 28 g Carbohydrate (2 g Fibre, 2 g Sugar); 7 g Protein; 620 mg Sodium

Baked Stuffed Eggplant

Stuffed eggplant is a versatile vegetarian main that is relatively simple to make and hearty enough to satisfy even the largest appetites. We've gone with a Mediterranean-inspired filling for our eggplant, but the possibilities are endless.

Eggplants (about 1 lb., 454 g, each)	2	2
Lemon juice	1 tbsp.	15 mL
Olive oil	1 tbsp.	15 mL
Olive oil	2 tsp.	10 mL
Chopped onion	1 cup	250 mL
Dried thyme	1 tsp.	5 mL
Dried oregano	1 tsp.	5 mL
Salt	1 tsp.	5 mL
Pepper	1/2 tsp.	2 mL
Garlic cloves, minced	2	2
(or 1/2 tsp., 2 mL, powder)		
Capers	1/4 cup	60 mL
Marinara sauce	1 1/2 cups	375 mL
Large egg, fork-beaten	1	1
Cherry tomatoes, cut in half	1 cup	250 mL
Grated mozzarella cheese	2 cups	500 mL
Olive oil	1 tbsp.	15 mL
Fresh thyme, for garnish		
Capers, for garnish		

Cut eggplants in half lengthwise. Carefully scoop out flesh leaving a 1/2 inch (12 mm) border on bottom and sides. Transfer flesh to a cutting board and chop. Place in a medium bowl and toss with lemon juice. Set aside. Brush eggplants with first amount of oil.

Heat a 14 inch (35 cm) cast iron skillet to medium. Add second amount of oil. Add onion and cook, stirring occasionally, until browned, about 6 to 7 minutes. Stir in chopped eggplant, thyme, oregano, salt and pepper and cook, stirring often, until eggplant has softened, about 10 to 12 minutes.

Add garlic and capers and cook, stirring often, until fragrant, about 2 minutes. Add marinara sauce and stir well. Transfer to a medium bowl and stir in egg and cherry tomatoes.

Divide filling evenly among eggplants and top with mozzarella. Wipe out skillet and brush with remaining oil. Place eggplants in skillet and bake in 350°F (175°C) oven for 50 minutes until eggplants are soft and cheese has melted. Garnish with thyme and capers. Makes 4 servings.

1 serving: 380 Calories; 21 g Total Fat (8 g Mono, 2.5 g Poly, 7 g Sat); 85 mg Cholesterol; 32 g Carbohydrate (10 g Fibre, 17 g Sugar); 16 g Protein; 1650 mg Sodium

Blistered Shishito Peppers

Shishito peppers originate from eastern Asian and look a lot like small, thin, wrinkled jalapeño peppers. Although they are much milder than their Central American cousins, you will find the odd shishito pepper that is spicy enough to make your eyes water.

Soy sauce	1/4 cup	60 mL
Brown sugar	1 tbsp.	15 mL
Garlic cloves, minced	2	2
(or 1/2 tsp., 2 mL, powder)		
Grated ginger root	1/2 tsp.	2 mL
Mirin	1/2 tsp.	2 mL
Salt	1/2 tsp.	2 mL
Olive oil	2 tbsp.	30 mL
Shishito peppers, cleaned and trimmed	2 cups	500 mL
(see Tip, page 26)		
Lemon juice	3 tbsp.	45 mL
Sesame seeds	2 tsp.	10 mL
Lemon wedges	4	4

Combine first 6 ingredients in a small bowl. Set aside.

Heat a 10 inch (25 cm) cast iron skillet to medium-high. Add oil. Add peppers and cook until slightly blackened, about 2 to 3 minutes per side. Stir in lemon juice and cook, stirring often, until lemon juice has almost evaporated. Add soy sauce mixture and cook, stirring, until liquid has almost evaporated. Remove from heat.

Sprinkle with sesame seeds and serve with lemon wedges. Makes 4 servings.

1 serving: 120 Calories; 8 g Total Fat (5 g Mono, 1 g Poly, 1 g Sat); 0 mg Cholesterol; 10 g Carbohydrate (2 g Fibre, 6 g Sugar); 3 g Protein; 1220 mg Sodium

Scalloped Potatoes

Thinly sliced potato nestled in a rich, creamy cheesy sauce, the perfect side for ham, pork chops or roasted or fried chicken. Although you could use russet potatoes, we prefer Yukon gold potatoes for this dish because they hold their shape better when cooked, giving the dish a creamier texture.

Medium potatoes, peeled and quartered lengthwise	4	4
Butter (or hard margarine)	1/4 cup	60 mL
Chopped onion	1 cup	250 mL
All-purpose flour	1/4 cup	60 mL
Salt	1 tsp.	5 mL
Pepper	1/4 tsp.	1 mL
Warm milk	2 cups	500 mL
Chopped fresh rosemary	2 tsp.	10 mL
Butter (or hard margarine)	1 tbsp.	15 mL
Grated Parmesan cheese	1/2 cup	125 mL

Cook potatoes in boiling salted water in a medium saucepan until tender. Drain and let stand until cool enough to handle. Cut into thin slices. Set aside.

Heat a 10 inch (25 cm) cast iron skillet to medium. Melt first amount of butter. Add onion and cook for 5 to 10 minutes, stirring often, until onion is softened. Add flour, salt and pepper. Cook, stirring, for 1 minute. Slowly add milk, stirring constantly until smooth. Cook, stirring, for 3 to 5 minutes until boiling and thickened. Whisk in rosemary. Remove from heat and pour sauce into a medium bowl.

Brush skillet with second amount of butter. Arrange potatoes in skillet in an overlapping spiral pattern and sprinkle with cheese. Pour half of sauce over top. Repeat layer with remaining potatoes, cheese and sauce. Bake, covered, in 350°F (175°C) oven for about 40 minutes until heated through. Remove cover and bake for 5 to 10 minutes until top is golden. Makes 6 servings.

1 serving: 300 Calories; 13 g Total Fat (3 g Mono, 0.5 g Poly, 8 g Sat); 35 mg Cholesterol; 37 g Carbohydrate (3 g Fibre, 7 g Sugar); 11 g Protein; 650 mg Sodium

Roasted Garlic and Root Vegetables

Roasting garlic mellows its pungent flavour and makes it sweeter—perfect for pairing with oven roasted beets, carrots and potatoes. If you have any leftover roasted garlic cloves, spread them on a piece of toast for the ultimate garlic bread.

Garlic bulb	1	1
Olive oil	1 tbsp.	15 mL
Olive oil	3 tbsp.	45 mL
Medium beets, peeled and cut into 1/4 inch (6 mm) wedges	2	2
Baby or small carrots, peeled and tip of greens kept on	8	8
Medium purple or red potatoes, cut into quarters	4	4
Balsamic vinegar	3 tbsp.	45 mL
Salt	1 tsp.	5 mL
Pepper	1/2 tsp.	2 mL
Finely chopped fresh dill	1 tbsp.	15 mL

Trim 1/4 inch (6 mm) from garlic bulb to expose tops of cloves, leaving bulbs intact. Pour oil over top. Wrap bulbs loosely in greased foil and bake in 375°F (190°C) oven for about 40 to 45 minutes until tender. Let stand until cool enough to handle.

Heat a 12 inch (30 cm) cast iron skillet to medium. Add remaining oil. Add beets, carrots and potatoes and toss to coat evenly with oil. Cook, stirring occasionally, until vegetables begin to brown, about 6 or 7 minutes.

Stir in balsamic vinegar and cook until vinegar is almost evaporated. Add salt and pepper and stir well.

Transfer skillet to 375°F (190°C) oven and roast for about 25 to 30 minutes, stirring every 8 minutes, until vegetables are soft. Remove from oven and stir in dill. Squeeze garlic cloves out of bulb, mash slightly and stir into vegetables. Makes 4 servings.

1 serving: 370 Calories; 14 g Total Fat (10 g Mono, 1.5 g Poly, 2 g Sat); 0 mg Cholesterol; 57 g Carbohydrate (7 g Fibre, 11 g Sugar); 7 g Protein; 700 mg Sodium

Garlic Chili Seared Green Beans

These green beans are a bit crispy and blackened on the outside but stay tender and juicy overall. If you prefer a bit more heat, add some extra chili garlic paste or crushed chilies.

Prepared vegetable broth	1/4 cup	60 mL
Soy sauce	2 tbsp.	30 mL
Rice vinegar	1 tbsp.	15 mL
Chili garlic paste (sambal oelek)	2 tsp.	10 mL
Granulated sugar	1 tsp.	5 mL
Dried crushed red chilies	1/2 tsp.	2 mL
Cooking oil	2 tbsp.	30 mL
Fresh green beans, trimmed	1 lb.	454 g
Thinly sliced red pepper	1 cup	250 mL
Thinly sliced carrot	1/2 cup	125 mL
Frozen peas, thawed	1/2 cup	125 mL
Garlic cloves, minced	2	2
(or 1/2 tsp., 2 mL, powder)		

Combine first 6 ingredients in a small bowl. Set aside.

Heat a 12 inch (30 cm) cast iron skillet or wok to medium-high. Add oil. Add green beans, red peppers and carrots and cook, stirring constantly, for 3 to 5 minutes until vegetables begin to brown.

Stir in peas and garlic. Cook, stirring constantly, until fragrant, about 2 minutes. Stir in soy sauce mixture and cook, stirring occasionally, until almost evaporated. Makes 6 servings.

1 serving: 90 Calories; 4.5 g Total Fat (3 g Mono, 1.5 g Poly, 0 g Sat); 0 mg Cholesterol; 10 g Carbohydrate (4 g Fibre, 4 g Sugar); 3 g Protein; 410 mg Sodium

Balsamic Charred Brussels Sprouts

Slightly salty from the bacon and tangy from the balsamic vinegar, these Brussels sprouts are nothing like the mushy mess you dreaded as a child. The cast iron skillet makes them beautifully crispy. For best results, use fresh sprouts, not frozen. Frozen sprouts retain a lot of water and will affect the texture of the dish.

Bacon slices	6	6
Olive oil	2 tbsp.	30 mL
Chopped onions	3/4 cup	175 mL
Brussels sprouts, cleaned, halved if large	2 lbs.	900 g
Water	3 tbsp.	45 mL
Garlic cloves, minced (or 1/2 tsp., 2 mL, powder)	2	2
Balsamic vinegar	1/4 cup	60 mL
Salt	1/2 tsp.	2 mL

Heat a 12 inch (30 cm) cast iron skillet to medium. Add bacon and cook until crispy, about 6 minutes. Transfer to a plate lined with paper towel to drain. Discard all but 1 tbsp. (15 mL) drippings from skillet. Chop bacon and set aside.

Reheat skillet to medium and add oil. Add onions and cook, stirring occasionally, until softened, about 5 minutes.

Add Brussels sprouts and cook, stirring occasionally, until beginning to char, about 10 to 15 minutes. Add water and cook, stirring often, until water has evaporated and sprouts are tender.

Add garlic and cook, stirring, until fragrant, about 2 minutes. Add bacon, balsamic vinegar and salt. Cook, stirring, until vinegar is reduced by half. Makes 8 servings.

1 serving: 220 Calories; 17 g Total Fat (8 g Mono, 2 g Poly, 4.5 g Sat); 20 mg Cholesterol; 13 g Carbohydrate (5 g Fibre, 4 g Sugar); 7 g Protein; 410 mg Sodium

Zucchini Fritters

Crispy on the outside with soft cheesy bits on the inside, these fritters make the perfect side dish. Pair them with some homemade tzatziki for dipping.

Shredded zucchini	2 cups	500 mL
Bread crumbs	1 cup	250 mL
Grated Parmesan cheese	1/2 cup	125 mL
Large eggs, fork-beaten	2	2
Garlic cloves, minced	2	2
(or 1/2 tsp., 2 mL, powder)		
Chopped fresh basil	2 tbsp.	30 mL
Salt	1/2 tsp.	2 mL
Pepper	1/2 tsp.	2 mL
Butter (or hard margarine)	1 tbsp.	15 mL
Cooking oil	1 tbsp.	15 mL

Place zucchini in a clean tea towel and squeeze as much liquid out as possible. Transfer to a large bowl and add next 7 ingredients. Mix until well incorporated. Divide into 8 portions.

Heat a 12 inch (30 cm) cast iron skillet to medium. Add half of butter and half of oil, and lower heat to medium-low. Once butter has melted, drop 4 portions of zucchini mixture into skillet. Press down lightly to form 3 inch (7.5 cm) rounds. Cook for 3 or 4 minutes per side until browned. Transfer to a plate lined with paper towel to drain. Cover to keep warm. Repeat with remaining butter, cooking oil and zucchini mixture. Makes 8 fritters.

1 fritter: 130 Calories; 7 g Total Fat (2.5 g Mono, 1 g Poly, 2.5 g Sat); 60 mg Cholesterol; 13 g Carbohydrate (0 g Fibre, 1 g Sugar); 6 g Protein; 440 mg Sodium

Cornbread

Somehow cornbread just tastes better when cooked in a cast iron skillet. Whether you slather it with butter or jam or serve it alongside a steaming bowl of chili, this cornbread is sure to please!

All-purpose flour	1 1/2 cups	375 mL
Yellow cornmeal	1 cup	250 mL
Granulated sugar	1/2 cup	125 mL
Baking powder	2 tsp.	10 mL
Baking soda	1 tsp.	5 mL
Salt	1/2 tsp.	2 mL
Large egg	1	1
Buttermilk (or soured milk, see Tip, below)	1 cup	250 mL
Butter (or hard margarine), melted	1/4 cup	60 mL

Combine first 6 ingredients in a large bowl. Make a well in centre.

Combine remaining 3 ingredients in a small bowl. Add to well. Spread in a greased 9 inch (23 cm) cast iron skillet. Bake in 350°F (175°C) oven for about 30 minutes until wooden pick inserted in centre comes out clean. Let stand in skillet for 5 minutes before removing to a wire rack to cool. Makes 12 servings.

1 serving: 190 Calories; 4.5 g Total Fat (1 g Mono, 0 g Poly, 2.5 g Sat); 30 mg Cholesterol; 32 g Carbohydrate (0 g Fibre, 8 g Sugar); 3 g Protein; 300 mg Sodium

Tip: To make soured milk, measure 1 tbsp. (15 mL) white vinegar or lemon juice into a 1 cup (250 mL) liquid measure. Add enough milk to make 1 cup (250 mL). Stir and let sit for 1 minute.

Buttermilk Biscuits

*If you like biscuits that are slightly crunchy on the bottom, flakey on top and
fluffy on the inside, then this is the recipe for you. Serve the biscuits as a side with
your favourite chili or stew, or offer them up for brunch or as a nice light snack.*

All-purpose flour	2 cups	500 mL
Granulated sugar	2 tbsp.	30 mL
Baking powder	4 tsp.	20 mL
Baking soda	1/2 tsp.	2 mL
Salt	1/2 tsp.	2 mL
Cold butter, cut into cubes	1/2 cup	125 mL
Buttermilk (or soured milk, see Tip, page 102)	3/4 cup	175 mL
Butter (or hard margarine), melted	2 tbsp.	30 mL

Combine flour, sugar, baking powder, baking soda and salt in a medium
bowl.

Cut cold butter into flour mixture until it resembles coarse crumbs. Stir in
buttermilk until moistened. Turn mixture onto a lightly floured surface and
knead until dough comes together. Pat down to 1 inch (2.5 cm) thickness.
Using a 2 inch (5 cm) biscuit cutter, cut into 12 circles.

Brush a 12 inch (30 cm) cast iron skillet with melted butter. Carefully add
biscuits to skillet and bake in 425°F (220°C) oven for 12 to 15 minutes, until
golden brown and a toothpick inserted in centre comes out clean. Serve
warm. Makes 12 biscuits.

*1 biscuit: 170 Calories; 10 g Total Fat (2.5 g Mono, 0 g Poly, 6 g Sat); 25 mg Cholesterol;
18 g Carbohydrate (0 g Fibre, 0 g Sugar); 2 g Protein; 330 mg Sodium*

Skillet Apple Pie

In this irresistible pie, tender cinnamon-flavoured apples are nestled between layers of flakey pastry. If the top crust browns too quickly, lay a sheet of foil over top of the pie to allow the bottom crust to finish baking. Serve with a dollop of ice cream for a special treat.

Pastry for 2 crust 9 inch (23 cm) pie

Butter (or hard margarine)	1/2 cup	125 mL
Granulated sugar	1 cup	250 mL
All-purpose flour	2 tbsp.	30 mL
Ground cinnamon	1/2 tsp.	2 mL
Sliced, peeled cooking apples	5 cups	1.25 L
such as McIntosh or Granny Smith		
Lemon juice	2 tsp.	10 mL
Granulated sugar	1/2 tsp.	2 mL

Divide pastry into 2 portions, making 1 portion slightly larger than the other. Shape each portion into a slightly flattened disk. Roll out large piece on a lightly floured surface to about 1/8 inch (3 mm) thick. Set aside.

In a 9 inch (23 cm) cast iron skillet, melt butter on medium heat. Remove from heat and brush butter over bottom and sides of skillet. Press pie crust in bottom and up sides of skillet.

Combine next 3 ingredients in a small bowl. Stir apples and lemon juice in a large bowl. Sprinkle with flour mixture and stir well. Spread in pie shell. Roll out smaller portion of pastry on a lightly floured surface to about 1/8 inch (3 mm) thickness. Dampen edge of pastry shell with water. Cover with remaining pastry. Trim and crimp decorative edge to seal.

Sprinkle with second amount of sugar. Cut several small vents into top to allow steam to escape. Bake on bottom rack at 350°F (175°C) oven for 45 to 55 minutes until golden and apples are tender. Cuts into 8 wedges.

1 wedge: 470 Calories; 27 g Total Fat (10 g Mono, 4.5 g Poly, 11 g Sat); 30 mg Cholesterol; 56 g Carbohydrate (3 g Fibre, 32 g Sugar); 3 g Protein; 320 mg Sodium

Chocolate Chip Brownies

Brownies cooked in a skillet? You bet! A cast iron skillet might not seem like an obvious choice for baking brownies, but the end result is rich and fudgy on the inside with a just the right amount of crispiness on the outside. Delicious!

Butter, softened	1/2 cup	125 mL
Dark chocolate	4 oz.	113 g
Unsweetened chocolate	1 oz.	28 g
Large eggs	2	2
Granulated sugar	1/2 cup	125 mL
Vanilla extract	1 tsp.	5 mL
All-purpose flour	1/4 cup	60 mL
Baking powder	1 tsp.	5 mL
Salt	1/4 tsp.	1 mL
Chocolate chips or chunks	1/2 cup	125 mL
All-purpose flour	1 tbsp.	15 mL

In a double boiler melt butter and both chocolates on medium-low. Stir until smooth. Set aside for 5 to 10 minutes to cool.

In a medium bowl cream together eggs, sugar and vanilla. Stir chocolate mixture into egg mixture until well combined.

Combine next 3 ingredients in a small bowl. Carefully stir into chocolate mixture until just combined.

Combine chocolate chips and flour. Fold into chocolate mixture. Divide batter evenly between 4 prepared 3 1/2 inch (9 cm) cast iron skillets. Place on a baking sheet lined with parchment paper. Bake in 350°F (175°C) oven for 20 to 30 minutes, until cooked through. Remove from oven and allow to cool before serving. Makes 4 servings.

1 serving: 700 Calories; 46 g Total Fat (7 g Mono, 1 g Poly, 29 g Sat); 165 mg Cholesterol; 71 g Carbohydrate (5 g Fibre, 54 g Sugar); 9 g Protein; 420 mg Sodium

Pear and Cherry Galette

To keep this galette nice and crispy, use a slotted spoon to transfer the fruit mixture to the skillet before baking; otherwise, your fruit mixture may include too much liquid and your pastry will be soggy.

All-purpose flour	1 1/4 cup	300 mL
Granulated sugar	2 tbsp.	30 mL
Salt	1/4 tsp.	1 mL
Butter (or hard margarine)	1/2 cup	125 mL
Ice water	1/4 cup	60 mL
Large egg yolks	2	2
Sliced pears	4 cups	1 L
Sweet cherries, pitted and halved	2 cups	500 mL
Lemon juice	2 tbsp.	30 mL
Vanilla extract	1 tsp.	5 mL
Brown sugar, lightly packed	1/2 cup	125 mL
Cornstarch	1/4 cup	60 mL
Ground cinnamon	1 tsp.	5 mL
Large egg, beaten	1	1

For the crust, combine flour, sugar and salt in a large bowl. Cut in butter until mixture resembles coarse crumbs.

Beat ice water and egg yolks together. Slowly add to flour mixture, stirring with a fork until mixture comes together. Add an extra spoonful of water, if necessary. Do not over mix. Turn onto a floured work surface and shape into a flattened disk. Wrap with plastic wrap and chill for 1 hour.

Combine pears, cherries, lemon juice and vanilla in a large bowl.

In a small bowl, combine brown sugar, cornstarch and cinnamon. Sprinkle evenly over fruit mixture and toss to distribute evenly. Let stand for 15 minutes.

Roll out dough to a 13 inch (33 cm) circle and transfer to a greased 10 inch (28 cm) cast iron skillet. Spoon filling onto dough with a slotted spoon, leaving a 2 1/2 inch (6.4 cm) border. Fold a section of edge up and over edge of filling. Repeat until pastry border is completely folded around filling. Brush pastry edge with beaten egg. Bake in 400°F (200°C) oven for about 30 to 35 minutes until pastry is golden and filling is bubbling. Cuts into 8 wedges.

1 wedge: 340 Calories; 14 g Total Fat (4 g Mono, 1 g Poly, 8 g Sat); 110 mg Cholesterol; 53 g Carbohydrate (4 g Fibre, 28 g Sugar); 4 g Protein; 95 mg Sodium

Cinnamon Buns

This recipe uses a special steam baking method to give the buns a dark crust and tender interior. Ice cubes are added to a hot pan in the oven along with the buns, and steam from the melting ice helps the buns cook to golden perfection.

Milk	1 1/2 cups	375 mL
Granulated sugar	1 tsp.	5 mL
All-purpose flour	1 tbsp.	15 mL
Envelopes of dry active yeast (1/4 oz., 8 g, each)	2	2
All-purpose flour	3 1/2 cups	875 mL
Granulated sugar	2 tbsp.	30 mL
Salt	1 tsp.	5 mL
Ground cinnamon	1/2 tsp.	2 mL
Large egg, room temperature	1	1
Butter (or hard margarine, softened	3 tbsp.	45 mL
All-purpose flour	1/3 cup	75 mL
Brown sugar, packed	1 cup	250 mL
Butter (or hard margarine), softened	1/2 cup	125 mL
All-purpose flour	1/3 cup	75 mL
Ground cinnamon	1 tbsp.	15 mL
Block of cream cheese (4 oz., 125 g), room temperature	1	1
Butter (or hard margarine), softened	3 tbsp.	45 mL
Vanilla extract	1 tsp.	5 mL
Icing (confectioner's) sugar	1 1/2 cups	375 mL

Combine milk and first amount of sugar in a heavy saucepan on medium. Cook, stirring, until milk is warm and sugar is dissolved. Remove from heat and add first amount of flour, stirring until smooth. Let stand for 5 minutes. Sprinkle yeast over top and let stand for 10 minutes. Stir until yeast is dissolved.

Combine next 4 ingredients in a large bowl and make a well in centre. Add egg, first amount of butter and yeast mixture. Mix until a soft dough forms. Turn out onto a lightly floured surface and knead 5 to 10 minutes, adding remaining flour 1 tbsp. (15 mL) at a time if necessary to prevent sticking, until smooth and elastic. Place in a large, greased bowl turning once to grease top. Cover with greased wax paper and a tea towel. Let stand in oven with light on and door closed for about 1 hour until doubled in bulk. Punch dough down and turn out onto a lightly floured surface. Knead for 1 minute. Roll out to a 9 x 12 inch (23 x 30 cm) rectangle.

Combine next 4 ingredients in a small bowl and sprinkle evenly over dough. Roll up jellyroll style, from long side and press down seam. Cut into 8 slices. Transfer, cut side up, to a prepared 14 inch (35 cm) cast iron skillet. Cover with greased wax paper and a tea towel. Let stand at room temperature for 30 minutes until doubled in size.

Heat an empty metal pan in 375°C (190°C) oven for about 10 minutes. Add 1 cup (250 mL) ice cubes to pan. Bake buns for about 30 minutes, until golden brown. Let stand for 10 minutes to cool.

For the icing, beat cream cheese and remaining butter in a small bowl until light and creamy. Beat in vanilla. Add icing sugar, 1/4 cup (60 mL) at a time, beating constantly until icing reaches a spreading consistency. Spread over cinnamon buns. Makes 8 buns.

1 bun: 710 Calories; 27 g Total Fat (6 g Mono, 1 g Poly, 16 g Sat); 95 mg Cholesterol; 105 g Carbohydrate (3 g Fibre, 52 g Sugar); 13 g Protein; 530 mg Sodium

S'mores Dip

Can't have a campfire? Why not bring this tasty treat inside by turning it into a delicious dip? Serve with extra graham crackers or you favourite cookies for dipping.

Butter (or hard margarine),	1/3 cup	75 mL
Graham cracker crumbs	1 1/4 cups	300 mL
Granulated sugar	2 tbsp.	30 mL
Chocolate chips	2 cups	500 mL
Regular-sized marshmallows	25	25
Graham crackers, optional		

Melt butter in a small saucepan on low heat. Remove from heat and stir in crumbs and sugar. Mix well. Press firmly into a greased 9 inch (23 cm) cast iron skillet, going up sides slightly. Bake in 350°F (180°C) oven for about 10 minutes, until slightly firm.

Pour chocolate chips onto crust and spread out. Arrange marshmallows close together over chocolate chips. Bake in 425°F (220°C) oven for 3 to 4 minutes or until marshmallows are plumped up and lightly brown on top. Set aside to cool slightly before serving. Serve with graham crackers for dipping. Makes 8 servings.

1 serving: 490 Calories; 25 g Total Fat (2 g Mono, 0 g Poly, 15 g Sat); 20 mg Cholesterol; 72 g Carbohydrate (5 g Fibre, 51 g Sugar); 5 g Protein; 190 mg Sodium

Beef Bourguignon

This classic dish originated in the Burgundy region of France, an area known for its excellent wine. It pairs well with hot cooked noodles.

All-purpose flour	1/4 cup	60 mL
Salt	1/4 tsp.	1 mL
Pepper	1/4 tsp.	1 mL
Round blade or sirloin steak, cut into 3/4 inch (2 cm) cubes	2 lbs.	900 g
Cooking oil	3 tbsp.	45 mL
Cooking oil	2 tbsp.	30 mL
Chopped onion	1 cup	250 mL
Chopped carrot	1 cup	250 mL
Garlic cloves, minced (or 3/4 tsp., 4 mL, powder)	3	3
All-purpose flour	2 tbsp.	30 mL
Prepared beef broth	2 cups	500 mL
Dry (or alcohol-free) red wine	1 1/2 cups	375 mL
Tomato paste (see Tip, page 83)	3 tbsp.	45 mL
Salt	1 tsp.	5 mL
Pearl onions, peeled (see Tip, page 117)	24	24
Bay leaves	2	2
Cooking oil	1 tbsp.	15 mL
Butter (or hard margarine)	1 tbsp.	15 mL
Quartered white mushrooms	2 cups	500 mL
Chopped fresh parsley	2 tbsp.	30 mL
Fresh thyme, for garnish		

Combine flour, salt and pepper in a plastic bag. Add beef cubes, a few at a time, and shake to coat. Transfer to a plate and repeat with remaining beef cubes until all are coated. Heat a cast iron Dutch oven to medium. Add 1 tbsp. (15 mL) of oil. Add a third of beef and cook until browned all over, about 6 to 8 minutes. Transfer to a bowl and set aside. Repeat with remaining oil and beef.

Heat second amount of vegetable oil in same Dutch oven on medium. Add onion and carrot and cook, stirring occasionally, until onions are softened, about 6 to 7 minutes. Add garlic and cook, stirring constantly, until fragrant, about 2 minutes.

Stir in beef. Add flour and cook, stirring constantly, for 2 minutes. Whisk in broth, red wine, salt and tomato paste, making sure there are no lumps. Stir in pearl onions and bay leaves. Cook, covered, 350°F (175°C) oven for 2 1/2 to 3 hours, stirring occasionally, until meat is fork tender.

Heat remaining oil in a medium cast iron skillet on medium. Add mushrooms and cook, stirring occasionally, until browned, about 7 to 9 minutes. Add mushrooms to Dutch oven and cook for 10 minutes. Sprinkle with parsley. Makes 6 servings.

1 serving: 500 Calories; 27 g Total Fat (14 g Mono, 4 g Poly, 6 g Sat); 85 mg Cholesterol; 20 g Carbohydrate (1 g Fibre, 5 g Sugar); 32 g Protein; 880 mg Sodium

Tip: To easily peel pearl onions, place them in a bowl and pour enough boiling water over top to cover. Drain and cut the ends off, then just slip the peels off.

Meatballs in Tomato Sauce

Serve the sauce and meatballs over spaghetti for a truly crowd-pleasing dish.

Large egg, fork-fork-beaten	1	1
Grated Parmesan cheese	1/3 cup	75 mL
Fine dry bread crumbs	1/4 cup	60 mL
Garlic clove, minced (or 1/4 tsp., 1 mL, powder)	1	1
Dried basil	1/2 tsp.	2 mL
Salt	1/4 tsp.	1 mL
Pepper	1/4 tsp.	1 mL
Lean ground beef	1 lb.	454 g
Olive oil	2 tbsp.	30 mL
Olive oil	1 tbsp.	15 mL
Chopped onion	1 cup	250 mL
Garlic cloves, minced (or 3/4 tsp., 4 mL, powder)	3	3
Dried oregano	1 1/2 tsp.	7 mL
Dried basil	1 tsp.	5 mL
Can of plum tomatoes (with juice) (28 oz., 796 mL), broken up	1	1
Can of crushed tomatoes (14 oz., 398 mL)	1	1
Granulated sugar	1 tsp.	5 mL
Salt	1/4 tsp.	1 mL
Pepper	1/4 tsp.	1 mL

For the meatballs combine first 7 ingredients in a large bowl. Add beef and mix well. Roll into 1 inch (2.5 cm) balls.

Heat a cast iron Dutch oven to medium heat. Add 1 tbsp. (15 mL) oil and half of meatballs. Cook until meatballs are browned on all sides, about 7 to 8 minutes. Transfer to a plate. Repeat with remaining meatballs and 1 tbsp. (15 mL) oil. Set aside. Makes about 32 meatballs.

For the tomato sauce reheat Dutch oven to medium. Add last amount of oil. Add next 4 ingredients and cook for about 7 minutes, stirring often, until onion is softened.

Add remaining 5 ingredients and bring to a boil. Reduce heat to medium-low and simmer, covered, for 15 minutes, stirring occasionally. Process with immersion blender until smooth (see Safety Tip, page 119). Add meatballs to sauce. Cook on medium heat, stirring occasionally, until heated through. Makes about 6 1/2 cups (1.6 L).

1 cup (250 mL): 320 Calories; 18 g Total Fat (10 g Mono, 1 g Poly, 6 g Sat); 80 mg Cholesterol; 16 g Carbohydrate (3 g Fibre, 7 g Sugar); 19 g Protein; 780 mg Sodium

Safety Tip: Follow manufacturer's instructions for processing hot liquids.

Goulash Soup

Goulash is a Hungarian soup or stew made with a variety of meat and vegetables, seasoned with paprika. The word "goulash" comes from the Hungarian guylás, meaning "herdsman." The stew was popular among herdsman on the Hungarian plains because all the ingredients, including wild vegetables such as onion, were easily found.

All-purpose flour	2 tbsp.	30 mL
Paprika	1 tsp.	5 mL
Pepper	1/2 tsp.	2 mL
Stewing beef, trimmed of fat, cut into 1 inch (2.5 cm) cubes	1 lb.	454 g
Cooking oil	1 tbsp.	15 mL
Chopped onion	1 cup	250 mL
Water	1/4 cup	60 mL
Garlic clove, minced (or 1/4 tsp., 1 mL, powder)	1	1
Prepared beef broth	4 cups	1 L
Caraway seed	1 tsp.	5 mL
Can of diced tomatoes (14 oz., 398 mL), with juice	1	1
Diced carrot	1 cup	250 mL
Diced yellow turnip	1 cup	250 mL
Diced peeled potato	1 cup	250 mL

Measure first 3 ingredients into a large resealable freezer bag. Add beef, seal bag and toss until coated.

Heat a cast iron Dutch oven to medium-high. Add oil. Add beef and cook, stirring constantly, for 3 to 4 minutes until browned. Reduce heat to medium.

Add next 3 ingredients and cook, scraping any brown bits from bottom of pan, until onion starts to soften, about 5 to 10 minutes.

Add broth and caraway seed and bring to a boil. Reduce heat to medium-low. Simmer, partially covered, for about 45 minutes, stirring occasionally, until beef is tender.

Add remaining 4 ingredients and bring to a boil. Cook, partially covered, for about 30 minutes, stirring occasionally, until vegetables are tender. Makes 4 servings.

1 serving: 310 Calories; 12 g Total Fat (5 g Mono, 1.5 g Poly, 3 g Sat); 55 mg Cholesterol; 22 g Carbohydrate (3 g Fibre, 7 g Sugar); 30 g Protein; 1110 mg Sodium

Coffee and Chocolate Braised Short Ribs

Short ribs have not always been the darling staple of top restaurants. This cut of meat has lots of fat, bone and connective tissue and was once considered "what was left" after the choice cuts of beef were taken. However, some simple kitchen magic entailing trimming and a long, moist cooking method results in meat that is tender, rich and tasty. Use any good, strong coffee that is not too bitter and combine it with your favourite dark chocolate for a unique dish that will have your friends coming back for more. Serve with potatoes.

Olive oil	1/4 cup	60 mL
Beef short ribs	5 lbs.	2.3 kg
Sea salt	2 tsp.	10 mL
Pepper	1 tsp.	5 mL
Chopped large onion	1	1
Chopped large red pepper	1	1
Finely chopped large jalapeño pepper, seeded (see Tip, page 26)	1	1
Garlic cloves, minced (or 1 tsp., 5 mL, powder)	4	4
Dark brown sugar	2 tbsp.	30 mL
Ancho chili powder	2 tbsp.	30 mL
Fresh chopped oregano	1/4 cup	60 mL
Cumin	1 tsp.	5 mL
Strong coffee	2 cups	500 mL
Can of diced tomatoes (28 oz., 796 mL), with juice	1	1
Tomato paste (see Tip, page 83)	1 tbsp.	15 mL
Dark, unsweetened chocolate, at least 70% cocoa, shaved	1 cup	250 mL
Salt, to taste		
Pepper, to taste		
Chopped fresh cilantro	2 tbsp.	30 mL

Heat a cast iron Dutch oven to medium-high. Add oil. Season ribs with salt and pepper. Working in batches, sear short ribs in oil until nicely browned and transfer to a platter.

Reduce heat to medium and add onions and peppers to oil and drippings in Dutch oven. Cook, stirring, until onions are softened, about 6 to 7 minutes. Stir in garlic and cook until fragrant, about 1 minute. Add brown sugar, ancho chili powder, oregano and cumin and cook for 5 minutes. Stir in coffee, tomatoes and tomato paste and bring to a boil. Add short ribs and collected juices to Dutch oven and heat until boiling.

Bake, covered, in 300°F (150°C) oven until meat is very tender, about 1 3/4 to 2 hours. Stir in chocolate until melted and evenly distributed in sauce. Stir in salt and pepper and garnish with cilantro. Makes 6 servings.

1 serving: 770 Calories; 50 g Total Fat (20 g Mono, 1 g Poly, 20 g Sat); 150 mg Cholesterol; 34 g Carbohydrate (5 g Fibre, 25 g Sugar); 53 g Protein; 1470 mg Sodium

Osso Buco

This dish hails from Milan, where it is traditionally topped with gremolata and served over saffron rice . Outside of Milan, osso buco is often paired with polenta or mashed potatoes. Garnish with fresh parsley for an attractive presentation.

All-purpose flour	1 cup	250 mL
Salt	2 tsp.	10 mL
Pepper	1/2 tsp.	2 mL
Veal shank, cut into 2 inch (5 cm) lengths	3	3
Cooking oil	1/4 cup	60 mL
Large onion, cut into wedges	2	2
Medium carrots, sliced	5	5
Sliced celery	1 cup	250 mL
Medium red peppers, chopped	2	2
Garlic cloves, minced (or 3/4 tsp., 4 mL, powder)	3	3
Parsley flakes	1 tbsp.	15 mL
Dry (or alcohol-free) white wine	1 cup	250 mL
Prepared beef broth	1 1/2 cups	375 mL
Can of diced tomatoes (14 oz., 398 mL), with juices	1	1
Lemon juice	1 tbsp.	15 mL

Combine flour, salt and pepper in a resealable freezer bag. Add veal, a few pieces at a time, and shake to coat. Heat a cast iron Dutch oven to medium. Add oil. Add veal and cook until browned, adding more oil if necessary. Remove from Dutch oven. Cover and set aside.

Reduce heat to medium-low. Add onion, carrot, celery and red pepper and cook, stirring occasionally, until softened, about 5 minutes. Stir in garlic and parsley, and cook until fragrant, about 2 minutes.

Add next 4 ingredients and bring to a boil. Reduce heat to a simmer. Add veal and simmer for 5 minutes. Bake, covered, in 325°F (160°C) oven for about 2 hours until veal is fork tender, adding more liquid if necessary. Sauce should be thick when done. If too thin, remove veal and vegetables and boil sauce uncovered until thickened. Makes 8 servings.

1 serving: 370 Calories; 12 g Total Fat (6 g Mono, 2.5 g Poly, 2 g Sat); 130 mg Cholesterol; 23 g Carbohydrate (2 g Fibre, 6 g Sugar); 36 g Protein; 1040 mg Sodium

Cassoulet

Our recipe for this stew is much quicker to prepare than the traditional version. It smells wonderful as it is cooking and tastes great served with crusty bread.

Bacon slices, cut in half	6	6
Smoked ham sausage, cut into 3 inch (7.5 mm) pieces	3/4 lb.	340 g
Skinless chicken legs, with backs attached (about 11 oz., 310 g, each)	4	4
Salt	1 tsp.	5 mL
Pepper	1/2 tsp.	2 mL
Olive oil	2 tbsp.	30 mL
Olive oil	1 tbsp.	15 mL
Chopped onion	1 cup	250 mL
Chopped fennel	1 cup	250 mL
Garlic cloves, minced (or 2 tsp., 2 mL, powder)	2	2
Dry (or alcohol-free) white wine	1 cup	250 mL
Cans of cannellini beans (19 oz., 540 mL, each)	2	2
Prepared chicken broth	1 1/4 cup	300 mL
Can of crushed tomatoes (14 oz., 398 mL)	1	1
Tomato paste (see Tip, page 83)	2 tbsp.	30 mL
Ground thyme	1 tsp.	5 mL
Bay leaf	1	1
Chopped fresh parsley	2 tbsp.	30 mL

Heat cast iron Dutch oven to medium. Add bacon and cook until almost crisp. Transfer to a plate lined with paper towel and set aside. Reserve drippings in pan. Add sausage and cook until browned on all sides, about 5 minutes. Transfer to plate with bacon.

Sprinkle chicken with salt and pepper. Reheat Dutch oven to medium. Add first amount of oil. Add chicken legs and cook until browned on all sides, about 6 minutes. Transfer to a plate and set aside.

Reheat Dutch oven to medium. Add second amount of oil. Add onions and fennel and cook, stirring often, until onion begins to soften, about 2 minutes. Add garlic and cook, stirring often, until fragrant, about 2 minutes.

Slowly add wine, stirring constantly and scraping any brown bits from bottom of Dutch oven. Cook for about 5 minutes, stirring often, until fennel is softened. Add sausage, bacon and chicken to Dutch oven.

Stir in next 6 ingredients. Bake covered, in a 300°F (150°C) oven for about 2 hours, until chicken and sausage are tender and cooked through. Stir in bacon and cook, covered, for 20 to 30 minutes. Discard bay leaf. Garnish with parsley. Makes 8 servings.

1 serving: 750 Calories; 44 g Total Fat (20 g Mono, 6 g Poly, 13 g Sat); 175 mg Cholesterol; 34 g Carbohydrate (9 g Fibre, 8 g Sugar); 50 g Protein; 1790 mg Sodium

Blackberry Pork Loin

For a perfect combination of savoury and sweet, elevate your pork tenderloin from tasty to amazing with this homemade blackberry sauce.

Boneless pork loin roast	2 1/2 lbs.	1.1 kg
Salt	1 tsp.	5 mL
Pepper	1/2 tsp.	2 mL
Olive oil	2 tbsp.	30 mL
Fresh (or frozen, thawed) blackberries	2 cups	500 mL
Granulated sugar	1/4 cup	60 mL
Water	1/4 cup	60 mL
Apple brandy	2 tbsp.	30 mL
Apple cider	1/2 cup	125 mL
Grainy mustard	2 tbsp.	30 mL

Season pork loin roast with salt and pepper. Heat a cast iron Dutch oven to medium. Add oil. Cook pork loin until browned on all sides, about 5 to 6 minutes per side. Bake, covered, in 450°F (230°C) oven for 10 minutes. Reduce heat to 350°F (175°C) and cook for 20 minutes.

In a medium cast iron skillet combine blackberries, sugar and water and bring to a boil. Add apple brandy and cook for about 5 minutes, scraping any brown bits from bottom of skillet. Stir in apple cider and mustard. Simmer until reduced by three-quarters, about 10 minutes. Brush glaze on pork loin and roast for 10 to 15 minutes, until internal temperature reaches 150°F (65°C). Let pork loin rest, covered, for 15 minutes. Slice pork and drizzle sauce over slices before serving. Makes 6 servings.

1 serving: 380 Calories; 15 g Total Fat (8 g Mono, 1.5 g Poly, 4 g Sat); 105 mg Cholesterol; 16 g Carbohydrate (3 g Fibre, 13 g Sugar); 42 g Protein; 540 mg Sodium

Roasted Lamb with Pomegranate Reduction

The reduction of pomegranate juice not only intensifies the flavour of the fruit, originally from the Middle East, but also balances the rich earthiness of the lamb, creating a feast of pleasing contrasts.

Pomegranate juice	3 cups	750 mL
Boneless leg of lamb roast, fat and sinews trimmed	3 lbs.	1.4 kg
Chopped fresh oregano	1/4 cup	60 mL
Garlic cloves, minced (or 1 1/4 tsp., 6 mL, powder)	5	5
Seasoned salt	2 tsp.	10 mL
Coarsely ground pepper	2 tsp.	10 mL
Olive oil	2 tbsp.	30 mL

Sprigs of fresh oregano, for garnish

Gently boil pomegranate juice in a saucepan on medium heat until reduced to about 1/2 cup (125 mL).

Place lamb on a cutting board flesh side up. Combine next 4 ingredients and rub half over inside of lamb. Roll lamb from short side. Tie tightly with butcher's twine in about 3 places. Chill, covered, for 2 hours.

Heat a cast iron Dutch oven to medium. Add oil. Add lamb and cook until browned on all sides, about 8 to 10 minutes. Pour off fat. Spread remaining oregano mixture over top of lamb. Cook in a 325°F (160°C) oven for 1 to 1 1/4 hours, until internal temperature reaches 145°F (63°C) for medium-rare or until lamb reaches desired doneness. Transfer to a cutting board and tent with foil. Let stand for 10 minutes.

Remove butcher twine and cut lamb diagonally, across the grain, into thin slices. Serve with pomegranate reduction. Garnish with oregano. Makes 8 servings.

1 serving: 420 Calories; 24 g Total Fat (10 g Mono, 1 g Poly, 12 g Sat); 130 mg Cholesterol; 15 g Carbohydrate (0 g Fibre, 14 g Sugar); 32 g Protein; 460 mg Sodium

Chicken Pot Pie

With its chunks of tender chicken and vegetables topped with a rich, flakey pastry crust, this dish is sure to please the whole family. A perfect way to use up any leftover chicken.

Diced potatoes, peeled	2 cups	500 mL
Sliced carrots	2 cups	500 mL
Diced cooked chicken (see Tip, page 133)	4 cups	1L
Butter (or hard margarine)	1/3 cup	75 mL
Chopped onion	2 cups	500 mL
Garlic cloves, minced	2	2
(or 1/2 tsp., 2 mL, powder)		
All-purpose flour	1/3 cup	75 mL
Warm prepared chicken broth	2 cups	500 mL
Warm milk	1/2 cup	125 mL
Dried thyme	2 tsp.	10 mL
Salt	1 tsp.	5 mL
Pepper	1 tsp.	5 mL
Ground nutmeg	1/4 tsp.	1 mL
Chopped tomatoes	1 cup	250 mL
Frozen peas	1 cup	250 mL
Pastry for 9 inch (23 cm) deep dish pie shell		

Place potatoes and carrots in a pan with just enough water to cover. Heat over medium-low until just soft, about 15 minutes. Drain and transfer to a bowl. Stir in chicken and set aside.

Heat a cast iron Dutch oven to medium. Add butter and heat until it melts. Add onion and cook, stirring frequently until softened, about 5 minutes. Stir in garlic and cook until fragrant, about 2 minutes. Lower heat to low. Add flour and cook, stirring constantly, for 2 minutes.

Slowly whisk in chicken broth and milk, whisking to prevent lumps. Cook, stirring, until slightly thickened. Whisk in thyme, salt, pepper and nutmeg. Cook, stirring frequently, until thickened.

Remove from heat and add chicken mixture, tomatoes and peas. Stir well. Roll out pastry about 1/2 inch (12 mm) larger than Dutch oven. Place over chicken mixture, pressing edge of pastry up sides of Dutch oven. Cut 3 or 4 small slits in pastry to allow steam to escape. Bake, uncovered, in 400°F (200°C) oven for about 30 minutes until pastry is golden. Makes 8 servings.

1 serving: 450 Calories; 22 g Total Fat (8 g Mono, 4 g Poly, 8 g Sat); 85 mg Cholesterol; 38 g Carbohydrate (4 g Fibre, 12 g Sugar); 26 g Protein; 790 mg Sodium

Tip: Don't have any leftover chicken? Start with 2 boneless, skinless chicken breast halves (about 4 oz., 113 g, each). Place them in a large frying pan with 1 cup (250 mL) water or chicken broth. Simmer, covered, for 12 to 14 minutes until no longer pink inside. Drain well and chop. Makes about 2 cups (500 mL) of cooked chicken.

Roasted Chicken

This roasted chicken, flavoured with thyme, rosemary and lemon, has golden, crispy skin and tender juicy meat. Serve with roasted or mashed potatoes and roasted or steamed carrots. Leftovers (if there are any!) make delicious sandwiches.

Whole chicken	5 lbs.	2.3 kg
Chopped fresh thyme	2 tsp.	10 mL
Chopped fresh rosemary	2 tsp.	10 mL
Kosher salt	2 tsp.	10 mL
Pepper	1/2 tsp.	2 mL
Medium lemon, cut in half	1	1
Small garlic head, cut in half horizontally	1	1
Sprigs of thyme	2	2
Sprigs of rosemary	2	2
Olive oil	2 tbsp.	30 mL
Large onion, thickly sliced	1	1
Dry (or alcohol-free) white wine	1/2 cup	125 mL
Prepared chicken broth	1/2 cup	125 mL

Sprigs of rosemary, for garnish
Sprigs of thyme, for garnish
Lemon wedges, for garnish

Pat chicken as dry as possible. Combine next 4 ingredients. Sprinkle half of mixture into cavity of chicken. Place lemon, garlic and herb sprigs into cavity.

Rub oil over surface of chicken. Tie wings close to body with butcher's string. Tie legs to tail. Transfer to an enameled cast iron Dutch oven.

Sprinkle chicken with rest of herb mixture. Scatter onion around chicken. Bake, covered, in a 400°F (200°C) oven for 20 minutes. Reduce heat to 350°F (175°C) and bake uncovered for 1 hour.

Add wine and broth to Dutch oven. Bake for 30 to 40 minutes until chicken reaches 185°F (85°C) in thickest part of chicken.

Remove chicken from oven. Cover with foil and let stand for 10 minutes. Carve chicken and spoon onions and pan juices over chicken. Garnish with rosemary, thyme and lemon slices. Makes 8 servings.

1 serving: 520 Calories; 14 g Total Fat (6 g Mono, 2.5 g Poly, 3.5 g Sat); 240 mg Cholesterol; 3 g Carbohydrate (0 g Fibre, 1 g Sugar); 88 g Protein; 780 mg Sodium

Chicken Gumbo

For this recipe you need to make a roux, which is a dark paste of flour and butter or oil and is used to thicken sauces and soups. For something a little different, try substituting pork or duck for the chicken, or Andouille sausage for the chicken sausage. Sprinkle with a few drops of hot sauce if you like a little heat.

Cooking oil	3 tbsp.	45 mL
Boneless, skinless chicken breast, cut into 1 inch (2.5 cm) pieces	2 lbs.	900 g
Chicken (or turkey) sausages, sliced (about 6 1/2 oz., 184 g)	6	6
Butter (or hard margarine)	1 cup	250 mL
Chopped onion	2 cups	500 mL
Chopped celery	2 cups	500 mL
Chopped green peppers	1 cup	250 mL
Chopped red pepper	1 cup	250 mL
Garlic cloves, minced (or 1 1/2 tsp., 7 mL, powder)	6	6
All-purpose flour	1 cup	250 mL
Prepared chicken broth	8 cups	2 L
Can of diced tomatoes (28 oz., 796 mL), with juices	1	1
Sliced okra	2 cups	500 mL
Barbecue rub	2 tbsp.	30 mL
Hot sauce	1/4 cup	60 mL
Dried oregano	1 tsp.	5 mL
Dried thyme	1 tsp.	5 mL
Cayenne pepper	1/4 tsp.	1 mL
Salt	1 tsp.	5 mL
Pepper	1 tsp.	5 mL
Cooked rice	6 cups	1.5 L

Heat 12 inch (30 cm) cast iron skillet to medium-high. Add oil. Add chicken and cook until golden brown. Transfer to a plate. Add chicken sausage slices and cook until golden brown. Transfer to same plate as chicken breast. Set aside.

Heat a cast iron Dutch oven to medium. Add butter. Add onions, celery and peppers, and cook until soft. Add garlic and cook, stirring constantly, until fragrant, about 2 minutes. Add flour and cook for 3 to 5 minutes, until you have a rich, dark brown roux.

Add next 10 ingredients and chicken to Dutch oven and simmer over low heat for 45 minutes to 1 hour, stirring occasionally. Ladle over rice and serve. Makes 8 servings.

1 serving: *960 Calories; 50 g Total Fat (19 g Mono, 4 g Poly, 22 g Sat); 290 mg Cholesterol; 74 g Carbohydrate (4 g Fibre, 11 g Sugar); 52 g Protein; 2950 mg Sodium*

Goose Stew

Domestic goose, unlike its wild counterpart, can be quite fatty, so make sure you remove the skin before cooking. In this stew, the long, slow cooking time in the Dutch oven makes the goose meat incredibly tender.

Skinless goose breasts, halved (about 20 oz., 540 g, total	2	2
Medium red onion, chopped	1	1
Medium red pepper, chopped	1	1
Medium green peppers, chopped	2	2
Medium carrots, chopped	2	2
Garlic cloves, minced (or 1/2 tsp., 2 mL, powder)	2	2
Can of diced tomatoes (28 oz., 796 mL), with juice	1	1
Sliced mushrooms	1 cup	250 mL
Salt	1/2 tsp.	2 mL
Pepper	1/2 tsp.	2 mL

Cut goose into bite-sized stew pieces and place in a cast iron Dutch oven. Add remaining ingredients and stir well. Cook, covered, in a 325°F (160°C) oven for about 1 1/2 to 2 hours, stirring occasionally, until goose is tender. Makes 4 servings.

1 serving: 450 Calories; 29 g Total Fat (13 g Mono, 4 g Poly, 7 g Sat); 110 mg Cholesterol; 20 g Carbohydrate (4 g Fibre, 12 g Sugar); 29 g Protein; 1030 mg Sodium

Paella

This classic Spanish rice dish gets its name from the Valencian word for the shallow pan it was traditionally cooked in. We find a cast iron Dutch oven is a great substitute for the traditional paella pan.

Cooking oil	2 tsp.	10 mL
Boneless, skinless, chicken thighs (about 3 oz., 85 g each) cut into 1 inch (2.5 cm) pieces	6	6
Chorizo sausage, cut into 1 inch (2.5 m) slices	4	4
Cooking oil	1 tsp.	5 mL
Chopped onion	1 cup	250 mL
Sliced red pepper	1 cup	250 mL
Garlic cloves, minced (or 1/2 tsp., 2 mL, powder)	2	2
Can of diced tomatoes (14 oz., 398 mL) with juice	1	1
Dry (or alcohol-free) white wine	3/4 cup	175 mL
Long grain white rice	1 1/4 cup	300 mL
Saffron threads (or turmeric)	1/8 tsp.	0.5 mL
Prepared chicken broth	1 3/4 cups	425 mL
Frozen, uncooked large shrimp, thawed (peeled and deveined)	1 lb.	454 g
Frozen peas	1 cup	250 mL

Heat a cast iron Dutch oven to medium. Add oil. Add chicken and cook for 3 to 4 minutes until browned on all sides. Transfer to a plate and set aside. Add sausage and cook for 5 to 10 minutes, turning occasionally, until brown on all sides. Transfer to same plate.

Reduce heat to medium-low. Add second amount of oil. Add onion and peppers and cook, stirring occasionally, for about 5 minutes until tender crisp. Add garlic and cook, stirring constantly, until fragrant, about 2 minutes. Increase heat to medium-high.

Stir in diced tomatoes and wine, and bring to a boil. Reduce heat to medium and cook for about 5 minutes, stirring occasionally and scraping any brown bits from bottom of Dutch oven.

Add rice and saffron, and stir until rice is well coated. Add broth, chicken and sausage, and bring to a boil. Reduce heat to a simmer and cook, covered, for 15 to 20 minutes, or until liquid is mostly absorbed. Stir in shrimp and peas.

Cook, covered, for another 10 minutes or until shrimp is pink and curled and peas are cooked through. Makes 8 servings.

1 serving: 460 Calories; 19 g Total Fat (2 g Mono, 1.5 g Poly, 6 g Sat); 170 mg Cholesterol; 33 g Carbohydrate (2 g Fibre, 5 g Sugar); 35 g Protein; 720 mg Sodium

Clam Chowder

An east coast favourite, chowder as we know it today is a thick, creamy soup frequently but not always made with seafood, as well as potatoes, onions and celery. The word "chowder" comes from the French chaudière, meaning "cauldron" or "kettle," which was also the name of a type of cast iron stock pot. In the fishing villages of 16th-century Brittany, fishermen would contribute part of their day's catch to a community chaudière. Villagers added vegetables, hard-baked biscuits and whatever else was on hand, such as butter or cream, with everyone getting a share of the soup. The practice came to Newfoundland with Breton cod fishermen, and from there it spread to the Maritimes. Following the British siege of Port Royal in 1710 and the subsequent Acadian expulsion from the Maritimes, the recipe spread south to New England.

Cans of clams (5 oz., 140 g, each), drained with juice reserved	3	3
Cubed potatoes	2 cups	500 mL
Water	1/2 cup	125 mL
Butter (or hard margarine)	3/4 cup	175 mL
Chopped onion	1 cup	250 mL
Diced celery	1 cup	250 mL
All-purpose flour	3/4 cup	175 mL
Warm milk	2 cups	500 mL
Warm heavy cream	1 cup	250 mL
Dried thyme	1 tsp.	5 mL
Salt	1 tsp.	5 mL
White pepper	1 tsp.	5 mL

Heat a 12 inch (30 cm) skillet to medium. Add juice from clams, potato cubes and water, and cook until potatoes soften, about 8 to 10 minutes.

Heat a cast iron Dutch oven to medium. Add butter and heat until melted. Add onions and celery, and cook until softened, about 5 minutes.

Add flour and cook, stirring, for 2 minutes. Reduce heat to low. Whisk in milk and cream until no lumps remain. Cook for 10 to 15 minutes, stirring constantly to prevent sticking.

Add potato mixture, clams, thyme, salt and pepper. Simmer, covered, for 10 minutes until chowder is smooth and creamy, stirring occasionally. Makes 4 servings.

1 serving: 640 Calories; 47 g Total Fat (12 g Mono, 2 g Poly, 30 g Sat); 140 mg Cholesterol; 44 g Carbohydrate (3 g Fibre, 10 g Sugar); 11 g Protein; 1180 mg Sodium

Port Royal Kitchen

Cioppino with Fennel and Saffron

Cioppino is an Italian seafood stew whose North American roots are thought to have originated in the San Francisco Bay area when Italian immigrants from Genoa replaced traditional Genoese ingredients with the fresh fish available to them on the West Coast. It is traditional to serve cioppino with polenta and a bottle of Chianti.

Snapper fillet, cleaned	2 lbs.	900 g
Fresh shrimp, tails on	1 lb.	454 g
Clams	1/2 lb.	225 g
Mussels (see Tip, page 145)	1/2 lb.	225 g
Scallops	1/2 lb.	225 g
Crab, cooked, cleaned and cracked	1	1
Extra virgin olive oil	2 tbsp.	30 mL
Small onion, minced	1	1
Medium fennel bulb, diced	1	1
White (or alcohol-free) wine	1 cup	250 mL
Garlic cloves, minced	3	3
(or 3/4 tsp., 4 mL, powder)		
Zest from half an orange, minced		
Pinch of saffron, or to taste,		
dissolved in 1/4 cup (60 mL) warm stock		
Tomato sauce	4 cups	1 L
Fish stock	3 cups	750 mL
Salt, to taste		
Pepper, to taste		
Fresh basil	1/2 cup	125 mL

Wash all fish and seafood, except crab, and pat dry.

Heat a cast iron Dutch oven to medium. Add oil. Add onion and cook, stirring often, until softened. Add fennel and cook, stirring often, for 5 minutes.

Add wine and garlic, and simmer for 10 minutes. Stir in orange zest, saffron, tomato sauce and stock, and simmer for 10 minutes. Nestle fish fillets and seafood into sauce, making sure to cover them with liquid. Cover, bring back to a simmer on medium-high and cook until clams and mussels open, about 10 to 12 minutes. Season with salt and pepper. Serve hot in warmed bowls, garnished with fresh basil. Makes 6 servings.

1 serving: *520 Calories; 11 g Total Fat (4.5 g Mono, 2.5 g Poly, 2 g Sat); 230 mg Cholesterol; 18 g Carbohydrate (3 g Fibre, 6 g Sugar); 75 g Protein; 2050 mg Sodium*

Tip: Use your fresh mussels within 24 hours of purchasing them. The best way to store fresh mussels is to put them in a colander and place the colander into a bowl. Cover the mussels with ice and then with a damp towel. The mussels will stay very cool and have good air circulation, without being submerged (or drowned) in water.

Black Bean Chili

Everyone loves a good chili! Feel free to substitute ground beef for the plant-based ground if you don't need this dish to be vegetarian. Pair this chili with a fresh French baguette or homemade loaf of sour dough bread.

Cooking oil	2 tsp.	10 mL
Plant-based ground	1 lb.	454 g
Chopped onion	1 1/2 cups	375 mL
Chopped celery	1/2 cup	125 mL
Chili powder	1 tbsp.	15 mL
Dried oregano	2 tsp.	10 mL
Garlic clove, minced	1	1
(or 1/4 tsp., 1 mL, powder)		
Can of stewed tomatoes (14 oz., 398 mL)	1	1
Chopped red pepper	1 1/2 cups	375 mL
Kernel corn	1 cup	250 mL
Can of tomato sauce (7 1/2 oz., 213 mL)	1	1
Hot pepper sauce	1/2 tsp.	2 mL
Can of black beans (19 oz., 540 mL), rinsed and drained	1	1
Sliced green onion	1/4 cup	60 mL
Grated sharp Cheddar cheese	1/2 cup	125 mL
Chopped fresh cilantro or parsley (optional)	2 tbsp.	30 mL

Heat a cast iron Dutch oven to medium. Add oil. Add plant-based ground and cook for about 3 to 5 minutes.

Add onion and celery and cook for about 10 minutes, stirring often, until onion is softened. Add next 3 ingredients and cook, stirring, for about 1 minute, until fragrant.

Stir in next 5 ingredients and bring to a boil. Cook, covered, for 15 to 20 minutes to blend flavours.

Stir in beans and green onion, and cook for another 15 minutes until heated through.

Sprinkle with cheese and cilantro. Makes about 7 cups (1.75 mL).

1 cup (250 mL): 270 Calories; 6 g Total Fat (1.5 g Mono, 0.5 g Poly, 2 g Sat); 10 mg Cholesterol; 37 g Carbohydrate (9 g Fibre, 10 g Sugar); 22 g Protein; 810 mg Sodium

Pumpkin Risotto

This version of risotto makes a great lighter main course. If you are a mushroom fan, toss a few sautéed mushrooms on top. Grated Parmesan cheese is also a nice touch; just make sure to use a vegan Parmesan cheese if you want to keep this dish vegetarian.

Butter (or hard margarine)	3 tbsp.	45 mL
Olive oil	3 tbsp.	45 mL
Finely chopped onion	1/2 cup	125 mL
Diced pumpkin	1 cup	250 mL
Arborio rice	2 cups	500 mL
Dry (or alcohol-free) white wine	1 cup	250 mL
Warm prepared vegetable broth	4 cups	1 L
Warm pumpkin soup	2 cups	500 mL
Chopped fresh rosemary	1 tbsp.	15 mL
Salt	1 tsp.	5 mL
Pepper, to taste		

Heat a cast iron Dutch oven to medium. Add butter and oil and heat until butter melts. Add onion and pumpkin. Reduce heat to medium-low and cook until just soft, about 7 to 9 minutes.

Add rice and stir to coat all grains evenly. Add wine and cook, stirring, until only about one-third of wine remains.

Combine broth and pumpkin soup. Add 1 cup (250 mL) broth mixture to rice and cook until liquid is just absorbed. Repeat until all of broth mixture is used (see Note, below).

Remove from heat and stir in rosemary, salt and pepper. Makes 6 servings

Note: Risotto must be cooked over low heat and stirred frequently to achieve the "creamy" texture. The broth should be warm but not boiling hot. To make the risotto ahead, prepare the dish as indicated above but hold back on the last cup (250 mL) of broth mixture. Transfer risotto to a bowl and chill immediately. To reheat, warm it over low heat and add the remaining broth and seasonings.

1 serving: 310 Calories; 14 g Total Fat (6 g Mono, 1 g Poly, 6 g Sat); 20 mg Cholesterol; 32 g Carbohydrate (3 g Fibre, 4 g Sugar); 4 g Protein; 980 mg Sodium

Cheese Fondue

Cheese fondue is a combination of cheese, brandy or wine and seasonings heated until they turn into a delicious melty cheese dip. This dish works exceptionally well in a cast iron enamel Dutch oven. Serve with your favourite dippers, such as cubes of bread, cherry tomatoes, steamed broccoli or cauliflower, or boiled baby potatoes.

Grated Gruyere cheese	1 1/2 cups	375 mL
Grated Gouda cheese	1 1/2 cups	375 mL
Grated fontina cheese	1 1/2 cups	375 mL
Cornstarch	2 tbsp.	30 mL
Dry (or alcohol-free) white wine	1 cup	250 mL
Garlic clove, minced	2	2
(or 1/2 tsp., 2 mL, powder)		
Lemon juice	2 tbsp.	30 mL
Ground nutmeg	1/4 tsp.	1 mL
Worcestershire sauce	1/4 tsp.	1 mL
Brandy	1 tbsp.	15 mL
Dijon mustard	1 tbsp.	15 mL

Combine cheeses and cornstarch in a large bowl, making sure all pieces are coated.

Heat a cast iron Dutch oven to medium-low. Add next 5 ingredients and bring to a simmer. Add cheese, 1/2 cup (125 mL) at a time, stirring well between each addition, until no lumps remain.

Whisk in brandy and mustard. Makes 6 servings.

1 serving: 380 Calories; 25 g Total Fat (7 g Mono, 1 g Poly, 16 g Sat); 95 mg Cholesterol; 6 g Carbohydrate (0 g Fibre, 2 g Sugar); 22 g Protein; 590 mg Sodium

Saffron Rice Pilaf

Saffron gives this pilaf a beautiful golden colour, while the cinnamon and coriander give a touch of warm spice. This dish pairs especially well with chicken, but it can also be served as a lovely vegetarian main.

Warm water	1 tbsp.	15 mL
Saffron threads	1/4 tsp.	1 mL
Water	8 cups	2 L
Salt	2 tsp.	10 mL
White basmati (or long-grain) rice	1 1/2 cups	375 mL
Butter (or hard margarine)	3 tbsp.	45 mL
Finely chopped onion	1/2 cup	125 mL
Chopped red pepper	1/2 cup	125 mL
Slivered almonds	1/4 cup	60 mL
Garlic cloves, minced	2	2
(or 1/2 tsp., 2 mL, powder)		
Cinnamon stick (4 inches, 10 cm, long)	1	1
Ground coriander	1/2 tsp.	2 mL
Salt	1/2 tsp.	2 mL
Chopped fresh cilantro	1 tbsp.	15 mL

Combine warm water and saffron in a small bowl. Set aside. Combine second amount of water and salt in a cast iron Dutch oven. Bring to a boil. Stir in rice and reduce heat to medium. Cook, uncovered, for about 15 minutes, stirring occasionally, until rice is tender. Drain and rinse with cold water. Drain well. Set aside.

Reheat Dutch oven to medium. Add butter and heat until melted. Add onion and peppers and cook, stirring often, for about 5 minutes until softened.

Add next 5 ingredients and saffron mixture. Cook, stirring often, until fragrant, about 2 minutes. Remove from heat. Add rice and stir well. Spread rice mixture evenly in Dutch oven. Bake, uncovered, in 375°F (190°C) oven for about 25 minutes until rice is heated through and edges are golden. Remove cinnamon stick. Garnish with fresh cilantro. Makes about 6 cups (1.5 L).

1/2 cup (125 mL): 130 Calories; 4 g Total Fat (1.5 g Mono, 0 g Poly, 2 g Sat); 10 mg Cholesterol; 20 g Carbohydrate (0 g Fibre, 0 g Sugar); 2 g Protein; 170 mg Sodium

Ratatouille

From its humble beginnings as a dish made by peasants in Provence, ratatouille has been elevated to a dish that graces restaurant menus throughout North America. The trick to delicious ratatouille is to get the eggplant and zucchini nice and caramelized before adding them to the tomatoes, and the cast iron Dutch oven does the job perfectly. This dish can be served as a main, with a fresh, crusty baguette for sopping up the juices, or as a side dish that pairs perfectly with grilled chicken or fish.

Chopped Asian eggplant (with peel)	3 cups	750 mL
Chopped zucchini (with peel)	3 cups	750 mL
Chopped red onion	1 cup	250 mL
Chopped red pepper	1 cup	250 mL
Olive (or cooking) oil	2 tbsp.	30 mL
Garlic cloves, chopped	2	2
(or 1/2 tsp., 2 mL, powder)		
Olive oil	2 tbsp.	30 mL
Chopped tomato	2 cups	500 mL
Can of tomato sauce (7 1/2 oz., 213 mL)	1	1
Dried dill weed	1 tsp.	5 mL
Grated lemon zest (see Tip, page 60)	1 tsp.	5 mL
Salt	1/2 tsp.	2 mL
Pepper	1/4 tsp.	1 mL
Chopped fresh basil	2 tbsp.	30 mL
Lemon juice	2 tbsp.	30 mL

Toss first 6 ingredients in a large bowl. Heat a cast iron Dutch oven to medium-low. Add cooking oil. Add vegetables and cook for about 10 minutes, stirring occasionally, until vegetables start to brown. Transfer Dutch oven to 425°F (220°C) oven and cook, covered, for about 25 minutes, stirring occasionally, until vegetables start to soften.

Stir in next 6 ingredients. Cook, covered, for 15 minutes, stirring occasionally.

Stir in basil and lemon juice. Makes about 6 cups (1.5 L).

1/2 cup (125 mL): 70 Calories; 4.5 g Total Fat (3.5 g Mono, 0.5 g Poly, 0.5 g Sat); 0 mg Cholesterol; 7 g Carbohydrate (2 g Fibre, 3 g Sugar); 1 g Protein; 200 mg Sodium

Sourdough Bread

This sourdough bread takes a bit of advance planning and a fair amount of time to make, but it is well worth it. Cooking sourdough in cast iron gives the bread that highly sought-after crispy crust.

Water	7 tbsp.	100 mL
Quick sourdough starter (see Note, below)	1 cup	250 mL
White bread flour	1 1/2 cups	375 mL
Water	7 tbsp.	100 mL
White bread flour	1 1/2 cups	375 mL
Whole wheat bread flour	1/2 cup	125 mL
Salt	1 tsp.	5 mL
Granulated sugar	1 tsp.	5 mL
White bread flour	1 tbsp.	15 mL

In a large bowl combine water, sourdough starter and first amount of white bread flour to form a dough that is too soft to knead. Cover with plastic wrap and set aside at room temperature for at least 12 hours.

Spoon remaining water over dough and add next 4 ingredients. Combine carefully to form a ball. Cover with plastic wrap and a tea towel and allow to rise for about 2 hours. Transfer dough to a lightly floured surface. Punch down gently and carefully knead dough for about 10 minutes. Shape into a ball and place in a 5 to 6 quart (5 to 6 L) cast iron Dutch oven lined with parchment paper and lightly dusted with flour. Cover with well-oiled plastic wrap. Set aside for about 2 hours or until it has doubled in size.

Dust loaf with remaining flour and cut a slit into it. Bake in 450°F (230°C) for 25 minutes, spraying oven 3 times with water in first 5 minutes. Reduce temperature to 400°F (200°C) and bake loaf for 10 minutes until golden and hollow-sounding when tapped on bottom. Transfer to a wire rack to cool. Cuts into 18 slices.

1 slice: 110 Calories; 0 g Total Fat (0 g Mono, 0 g Poly, 0 g Sat); 0 mg Cholesterol; 22 g Carbohydrate (1 g Fibre, 0 g Sugar); 4 g Protein; 130 mg Sodium

Note: To make a quick sourdough starter, at least 12 hours before you plan to make your bread combine 1 cup (250 mL) water, 1 cup all-purpose flour and 1/2 tsp. (2 mL) active dry yeast in a medium bowl. Set it in a draft-free area, allowing the starter time to develop. Remaining starter can be left on the counter for future use; it is best stored at 65° to 77°F (18° to 25°C). To strengthen and "feed" the starter, add 1/4 cup (60 mL) water and 1/2 cup (125 mL) flour every second day.

Index